Stephanie Barrat-Go
expert after first w
yoga teacher. She
and analytical body language and works as a trainer
for the Heinz Goldmann Foundation for Executive
Communication in Geneva and as a consultant for
companies all over Europe such as Shell and
Mercedes-Benz.

She has been interviewed by the BBC and lectures in French, Italian, English and German. The editor of a newsletter called *Effective Communicators*, aimed at top executives of large companies, she runs seminars on effective communication for various French ministries. Her previous books include *The Power Talk System*.

By the same author

THE POWER TALK SYSTEM
STAGE FRIGHT: HOW TO GET RID OF IT

How to Develop Charisma
& Personal Magnetism

STEPHANIE BARRAT-GODEFROY

Thorsons
An Imprint of HarperCollins*Publishers*

Thorsons
An Imprint of HarperCollins*Publishers*
77—85 Fulham Palace Road,
Hammersmith, London W6 8JB

Published by Thorsons 1993
1 3 5 7 9 10 8 6 4 2

© Stephanie Barrat-Godefroy 1993

Stephanie Barrat-Godefroy asserts the moral right to
be identified as the author of this work

A catalogue record for this book
is available from the British Library

ISBN 0 7225 2705 5

Typeset by Harper Phototypesetters Limited,
Northampton, England
Printed in Great Britain by
HarperCollinsManufacturing Glasgow

All rights reserved. No part of this publication may be
reproduced, stored in a retrieval system, or transmitted,
in any form or by any means, electronic, mechanical,
photocopying, recording or otherwise, without the prior
permission of the publishers.

Contents

Introduction: The Secret of Charisma ... 7

1 What Kind of 'Personality' Do You Have? ... 9
Test: You and Others ... 14

2 How Do You See Yourself? ... 17
Test: What Image Do You Have of Yourself? ... 18
Exercise: Free Yourself from the Past! ... 23
Exercise: Reprogramming ... 24

3 How to Develop Your Self-Confidence ... 27
Test: Are You an Optimist or a Pessimist? ... 30
Exercise: Self-Analysis ... 31
Exercise: Sort and File Your Failures ... 34

4 How to Overcome Your Shyness and Develop Your Courage ... 41
Test: What Kind of Shy Person Are You? ... 41
Exercise: Split Your Personality ... 47
Exercise: Cost-Benefit ... 52
Exercise: Inner Dialogue ... 53
Exercise: Survey ... 55

5 Improve Your Physical Appearance ... 59
Test: Your Physical Well-Being ... 59
Exercise: Improve Your Posture ... 65
Exercise for Relaxing the Shoulders ... 65
Exercise: The Ideal Walk ... 67
Test: Become Aware of Your Gestures ... 68
Exercise: Mime ... 69

Contents

Exercise: Staying Calm	70
Exercise: How to Develop an 'Irresistible Gaze'	74
Exercise: Strengthening the Eye Muscles	75
Exercise: How to Train Your Voice	77

6 The Keys to an Irresistible Appearance — 79

Exercise: Firm Up Your Thighs	85
Exercise: Improve Your Handshake	85
Exercise: Breathing	87
Test: Your Profile as a Dresser	87

7 How to Master Your Emotions — 93

Test: Emotivity	95
Exercise: Muscle Relaxation	101
Exercise: Visualisation	102
Exercise: Create a Mental Oasis	103
Exercise: The Spiral	105
Exercise: Counting	105
Exercise: Clouds	106
Preparatory Exercise: Breathing	109
Preparatory Exercise: Visualisation	109
Exercise: During the Event	110

8 How to Win the Confidence of Others — 113

Test: Do You Know How to Make Fast Decisions?	114
Exercise: Crisis Situations	117

9 How to Find—and Keep—Your Ideal Partner — 123

Test: What Kind of Partner Are You?	133

10 How to Become a Leader — 139

Test: Do You Possess Leadership Qualities?	139
Exercise: Job Inventory	148

Conclusion: Your Success Belongs to You — 159

INTRODUCTION

The Secret of Charisma

DEVELOP YOUR PERSONALITY

Why do some people have an immediate and positive effect on us, while others inspire indifference or even aversion?

Why do some people seem to be 'born under a lucky star' while others spend their entire lives vegetating?

Why are some people perpetually popular while others have no friends at all?

How could a young peasant girl of modest means raise an army, defy a king, rally her demoralized compatriots and put so much fear into her adversaries that they claimed she must be practising some kind of witchcraft? How could a little Corsican footsoldier, lacking physical stature or any kind of presence or bearing, become Emperor of half of Europe?

Did you know that 80 per cent of today's millionaires come from middle or lower-class backgrounds?

We are astounded by the achievements of historical figures, or by our contemporaries — colleagues, friends or relatives — who exert such a powerful influence on people that as soon as they open their mouths everyone seems to listen with rapt attention, unwilling to miss anything they have to say. These people possess an abundance of what is called charisma (derived from the Greek for 'divine grace'). To use a more material term, we could say that these people's personalities are 'magnetic'.

Charismatic persons seem to feel at ease wherever they go. They leave a trail of optimism and enthusiasm in their wake. They smile at you, and you forget about your problems and the dark clouds overhead. Their simple desires become our sacred commands.

Perhaps you've tried to study one of these people, to find out just what it is that makes them tick. And, of course, you failed. Why?

Quite simply because there is no mystery at all! People with charisma make no special effort to attract attention, respect, friendship or love. They just carry on being themselves.

Charisma has nothing to do with physical attributes. It springs from the heart, from the soul and mind of a person, and not from the body. Like all great powers, it is intangible.

Of course, the question you're asking yourself is, 'Is charisma an innate quality, or is it acquired?'

What do you think? If we look in the history books, we find thousands of charismatic figures, aside from Joan of Arc and Napoleon, who have all admitted that they worked extremely hard to acquire the magnetism they were able to exercise on the people around them. Sarah Bernhardt regularly suffered from terrible migraines before her performances. Lord Byron, Edith Piaf and Woody Allen were notoriously shy . . . but they all learned to conquer their shyness.

There's no reason why you can't do the same thing. You too can acquire a magnetic personality, that scintillating aura that adds weight to your every word, your every gesture, and seems to endow you with 'divine grace'.

How? By applying a method comprising a number of stages. First you evaluate your own personality. Are you shy? Are you assertive enough? Are you happy being who you are? Do you lack decisiveness? Are you paralysed by stage fright in front of a group? And so on.

Then you learn how to methodically eliminate all these weaknesses. You know you can, since so many have done it before. You don't have anything to be ashamed of. There are many confident, charismatic people today who, at one time, were just as timid and indecisive as you may be now.

All you need is a profound desire to succeed. Like all methods, this one requires steady application and perseverance. But the rewards, in terms of personality, development, are well worth the investment in time and effort that you will have to make.

CHAPTER ONE

What Kind of 'Personality' Do You Have?

How many times have you heard the word personality in the last month? Probably a dozen times, if not more. We say someone has a strong personality, or a likeable personality, or that someone is dull, and so on. We sometimes even say that someone doesn't have a personality at all.

But what is personality?

Personality is a mosaic of characteristics whose continual interplay conditions the various ways in which we behave. Therefore, our personality encompasses all our qualities and all our faults, and it is because of personality that each human being on the face of the earth is unique.

How is personality acquired? This is a question that philosophers and men of science have been pondering for centuries. Modern thinking generally maintains that personality is the result of certain hereditary factors upon which are grafted the external influences we experience, especially during our formative years.

But whatever hereditary, cultural or educational baggage you may be carrying around, you should know that you can change your personality, improve it, reinforce it, or round off any rough edges you may have.

SIX CHARACTERISTICS OF A LEADER

What kind of personality does a leader, someone who exudes charisma, have?

It seems that leaders possess six fundamental characteristics:

1 Simplicity

People with charisma are usually simple and modest. It's the people who fail continually who are arrogant. In a group, charismatic persons never try to attract attention by boasting about their talents or qualities, or by making a display of their virtues.

2 The ability to listen to others

A few years ago a popular magazine organized a contest. Readers had to concoct bits of philosophical or spiritual wisdom, in 25 words or less. One reader submitted the following gem: 'People who talk about themselves are bores, people who talk about others are gossips, but those who talk about you are brilliant conversationalists!'

It's so true. If you want to acquire a magnetic personality, you have to learn to encourage other people to express themselves, and to talk about themselves to you. Ask questions about their work, their hobbies, their families, and so on. Give them the opportunity to reveal themselves to you.

3 Self-confidence and assertiveness

Shyness, which we'll talk about in detail in chapter 4, is not necessarily a negative quality if it isn't exaggerated, in which case it's more like a healthy sense of propriety and reserve.

However, if your shyness prevents you from communicating with others, from assuming your rightful position in society, from meeting people with whom you believe you have something in common, from doing well on oral exams or showing your best side during job interviews, then you should do something about it. People with charisma are not overly shy, and if they were at one time, they have succeeded in overcoming it. We'll see how later on.

4 The ability to act decisively

This means not procrastinating — not putting off until tomorrow what you can do today. Charismatic people are neither negligent nor lazy. If procrastinating is one of your faults, you absolutely must get rid of it. Chapter 8 of this book is devoted to the problem.

Be honest: do you admire people who can't make up their minds, who always seem to be dragging their feet, and who have a pile of things they were supposed to do last week which they still haven't gotten around to? No, of course not.

5 Respect for your commitments

Does this seem obvious? Well, you may be surprised to learn how many people don't honour their commitments.

'Are you talking about minor or major commitments?' you ask. And that's exactly where you're going wrong. Because there are no minor commitments!

A commitment is always major, whether it's a promise to play tennis with someone, or to lend a substantial amount of money to a friend in need. You are judged just as severely on your punctuality at a dinner party as you are in repaying your debts. People with charisma are people you can count on. They are like rocks — steady fixed points in an unstable, changing universe.

6 Feeling good about yourself

Be careful! Feeling good about yourself doesn't mean you have to look like Robert Redford or Marilyn Monroe. Physical beauty has nothing to do with a person's magnetism. Never forget that.

President Roosevelt was an invalid; Cicero, according to historical descriptions, was afflicted with a repulsive physique; neither would Joan of Arc or Queen Elizabeth I have won any beauty contests. Many of society's most influential personalities have nothing physically attractive about them.

To feel good about yourself, you have to accept your physical qualities and defects, which are irremediable, and make the most of them. You can make this task easier by applying certain techniques which may enhance the way you appear to others. You'll find some ideas on this subject in chapters 5 and 6.

Now that you know what your personality *should* be like, it's time to find out what it *really* is like! Because it's only by knowing exactly who you are that you can try to change yourself and become the person you want to be.

HOW TO KNOW YOURSELF BETTER

Learning to know yourself calls for one essential quality: honesty.

You'll start by playing your own confessor and writing a list of your positive and negative characteristics.

Then you'll take a short test to determine if your relations with others leave something to be desired. Charismatic people are neither introverted nor extroverted. They have found a way to balance these two extremes in their relations with others.

A piece of advice: if you really think you can't be honest with yourself, if you're convinced that you're bound to leave out certain aspects of your personality that you'd rather not face up to, even if they're not especially negative, then I suggest having a sample of your handwriting analysed by a graphologist. A graphologist's report will spell out your positive and negative traits in black and white. You may be unpleasantly surprised, but if so you should remember that we're all capable of changing.

If you're not sure of yourself or of your own judgment, but you don't want to consult a graphologist, then ask someone close to you for help, someone whom you like but who also has a clear understanding of who you are. Don't go asking your boyfriend or girlfriend, whom you've known only for six months, to start listing all your faults. Don't ask your parents either. It's rare that a mother or father can judge their offspring objectively.

Turn to a childhood friend or an old friend of the family, a brother or sister, someone you've worked with for a number of years, an old professor whom you get along well with, or a therapist whom you've consulted at some point in your life.

What Kind of 'Personality' Do You Have?

Your qualities and faults
1 Start by listing your qualities. What ten qualities — or more — do you think you possess? Take some time to think about it, and then list a minimum of 10 responses on a piece of paper.
2 Now list the characteristics that you consider to be your major faults. Don't forget — be honest!

You may find the same characteristic in both lists, since a given quality, exaggerated to one extreme or another, can have both a positive and negative aspect.

Let's look at an example. You often help people out. You're therefore a helpful person, and that is an enviable quality. But what if you're so helpful it makes you incapable of saying no? You let people walk all over you, and that is a fault that can eventually ruin your life.

Another example: you're frank and direct with people. That's all very well. But maybe your frankness is a result of insensitivity. You may be ignoring the way you make other people feel, forgetting the old adage, 'Not all truths are worth telling.' Charismatic people are not hypocrites, far from it. However, they instinctively know when to remain silent in order not to hurt someone needlessly.

Above all, don't be hard on yourself when you read your list of faults — we've all got them!

Transform your weaknesses into strengths
Remember that nothing's perfect, and that perfection, if it did exist, would be singularly boring. And don't forget that you can transform your weak points into strengths.

Charismatic people are human beings just like you. They're far from perfect. Very often their charisma depends on what we would consider to be a defect: ambition pushed to its extreme (Napoleon), courage to the point of audacity (Alexander the Great), stubbornness (Joan of Arc), and so on.

What you consider a major fault in your own character may be the dominant quality in someone else whom you admire!

TEST: YOU AND OTHERS

Now complete this short test to find out how you are going to direct your efforts to change your relationship with other people.

1. In a group:
   a) *You often lead the conversation*
   b) *You prefer listening to others*

2. Which pastime do you prefer:
   a) *Dancing*
   b) *Reading*

3. Do you prefer to spend an evening in the company of:
   a) *One person*
   b) *A group of friends*

4. Where would you choose to go on vacation:
   a) *Acapulco*
   b) *A desert*

5. If someone says something that hurts you:
   a) *You close up like a clam*
   b) *You exhibit your pain, disappointment or anger immediately*

6. When you have to make a decision:
   a) *You trust your intuition and decide quickly*
   b) *You procrastinate*

7. Your relation to money can be described as follows:
   a) *You never know how much you have in your pocket*
   b) *You always check your bills to make sure there hasn't been a mistake*

8. Do you get the impression that other people extend invitations:
   a) *Out of politeness*
   b) *To make their parties more interesting*

9 Whenever some happy occasion occurs in your life:
   a) *You immediately tell everyone about it*
   b) *You say nothing because you think it doesn't concern or interest anyone but yourself*

10 To be happy you need:
    a) *A lot of people around you*
    b) *Your books and records*

Results

QUESTION	POINTS SCORED	
1	a = 3	b = 1
2	a = 3	b = 1
3	a = 1	b = 3
4	a = 3	b = 1
5	a = 1	b = 3
6	a = 3	b = 1
7	a = 3	b = 1
8	a = 1	b = 3
9	a = 3	b = 1
10	a = 3	b = 1

If you scored between 10 and 15 points:
You are an introvert.

You are rarely comfortable in a group, and you don't like meeting people. Social events seem superficial and a waste of time to you. You're probably very shy, preferring intellectual or physical activities which require no contact with other people. Obviously you won't be able to influence people by running away from them.

If you scored between 16 to 20 points:
You have a balanced personality.

You're well on your way towards obtaining a magnetic personality. You take pleasure in the company of others, but this doesn't prevent you from appreciating your quiet, intimate moments. You are liked by introverts as well as extroverts. Your relationships with the people around you are bound to be relaxed and mutually enriching.

If you scored between 21 to 30 points:
You are an extrovert.

You're overflowing with energy, and you're probably very ambitious. You constantly need to have people around you. It's possible that other people find you a little tiring, overbearing, even aggressive. You don't spend enough time with yourself, and it's likely that you need other people around all the time because you're insecure and lack self-confidence. Therefore a strategy for overcoming timidity and developing assertiveness will be just as important for you as someone who is introverted.

You are unique!
While recognizing that you may have to change certain aspects of your personality in order to make it more magnetic, it's important to accept yourself the way you are.

You are a totally unique collection of qualities and faults, of hereditary characteristics and acquired traits. No one else in the entire world is exactly like you on the inside, even though you may have an identical twin or a double who resembles you physically in every detail.

Don't forget this as you work with this book to attain a magnetic personality.

SUMMARY

You are now aware of the characteristics you must acquire in order to develop personal magnetism.

You have analysed the main characteristics which make up your own personality: you know yourself a lot better.

You now possess the basic elements you need to build your new personality, one that will open the door to a whole new life.

CHAPTER TWO

How Do You See Yourself?

You now know what you have to do to attract other people. You've also succeeded in determining, more or less precisely, what the main characteristics of your own personality are.

If you want other people to find you interesting, you first have to find yourself interesting. This is where 'self-image' comes in. The importance of a person's self-image is one of the major discoveries of modern psychology.

Charismatic persons project images which conform to reality. Their magnetism is, to a great extent, the result of this harmony, which becomes part of their being. They see themselves as they are, and have learned to work with their image. They radiate an aura of balance and psychological well-being, which makes them attractive to others.

Why not learn to correct the image you have of yourself? Don't worry, it's much easier than you might think at first glance. You just have to follow a few logical steps.

WHAT IS SELF-IMAGE?

Whether you're aware of it or not, you're carrying around a mental image of the way you believe you are. The key word here is 'believe'.

Where does this image come from?

A self-image is like a jigsaw puzzle — the individual pieces join together to form a whole. Just as jigsaw puzzles have two or three main types of pieces, identified by shape and colour, the image we have of ourselves is composed of multiple pieces which fit into each other, and which can be grouped, generally speaking, into three categories:

- *Body image* This, obviously, is the image we have of our bodies, based on the signals our body sends us. Since our body is ultimately the only tangible, concrete and visible entity we possess upon which we can base our judgment, it is the primary influence on our self-image.
- *Education* We are, to a great extent, the product of our education. Children who are suppressed and intimidated by parents or teachers will develop a strong tendency to underestimate themselves their whole life long, despite any personal successes they may achieve later on.
- *Interpersonal relations* We spend a lot of time comparing ourselves to others, especially during the first 30 years of our lives. So a good piece of advice if you want to be successful and attract the love and friendship of others is don't surround yourself with people who are depressed, defeatist, pessimistic, overly dependent, or who complain all the time. Seek out the friendship of people who are positive, optimistic, happy and independent.

TEST: WHAT IMAGE DO YOU HAVE OF YOURSELF?

The moment of truth has arrived. You don't have to rack your brain to figure out what kind of self-image you have. Just complete the following short test — as honestly as you can, of course!

1. When someone criticizes your attitude:
   a) *You feel guilty*
   b) *You respect the other person's opinion, without necessarily changing your behaviour*
   c) *You react by making any necessary adjustments*
2. In your relations with the people around you:

How Do You See Yourself?

    a) *You feel inferior*
    b) *You feel you are their equal*
    c) *You feel superior*

3 If someone gives you a compliment:
    a) *You accept gracefully and thank the person*
    b) *You consider the compliment unworthy of you*
    c) *You feel obliged to return the compliment*

4 When you're invited somewhere:
    a) *You consider it par for the course, because you know you're good company*
    b) *You think that you're just being asked to fill in for a missing guest*
    c) *You think that others need you to have a good time*

5 The past:
    a) *Preoccupies you almost completely*
    b) *Occupies a very small part of your thinking*
    c) *Occupies absolutely no place in your thoughts*

6 When someone tries to dominate you:
    a) *You submit*
    b) *You resist*
    c) *This couldn't happen, because you're the one who always dominates others*

7 During a group discussion:
    a) *You lead the discussion and try, using whatever means possible, to convince the others*
    b) *You accept the majority decision*
    c) *You express your point of view, but this doesn't prevent you from respecting other people's opinions*

8 When someone shows a desire to get to know you better:
    a) *You respond naturally*
    b) *You try to show your best side in order to impress the person*
    c) *You escape*

9 When you are promoted at work:
    a) *You tell yourself it was just a question of luck*

b) *You think that your boss has overestimated your abilities*
c) *You believe you merit the promotion*

10 You're invited to a barbecue party at a friend's house:
    a) *You constantly look for ways to help your host, in order to justify the invitation*
    b) *You decide you're not there to serve people*
    c) *Without being asked, you bring along a huge salad and a cake for dessert*

11 After a failure:
    a) *You see it as conclusive proof of your incompetence*
    b) *You analyse your behaviour in order to avoid committing the same mistakes again*
    c) *You automatically blame others*

12 You believe:
    a) *That you weren't born to achieve great things*
    b) *That you deserve the best things in life*
    c) *That you're perfectly suited to your present situation*

13 You find your exterior appearance:
    a) *Enormously pleasing*
    b) *Somewhat pleasing*
    c) *Acceptable*

14 Would you like to change the image you think you project?
    a) *Totally*
    b) *Partially*
    c) *Not at all*

15 Do you have confidence in your ability to achieve your goals?
    a) *Completely*
    b) *None at all*
    c) *It depends on others*

How Do You See Yourself?

Results

QUESTION	POINTS SCORED
1	a = 0 b = 5 c = 2
2	a = 0 b = 5 c = 2
3	a = 5 b = 2 c = 0
4	a = 5 b = 0 c = 2
5	a = 0 b = 5 c = 2
6	a = 0 b = 5 c = 2
7	a = 2 b = 0 c = 5
8	a = 5 b = 2 c = 0
9	a = 2 b = 0 c = 5
10	a = 0 b = 5 c = 2
11	a = 0 b = 5 c = 2
12	a = 0 b = 2 c = 5
13	a = 2 b = 0 c = 5
14	a = 0 b = 2 c = 5
15	a = 5 b = 0 c = 2

If you scored less than 20 points:

Your self-image is deplorable. Your general attitude is submissive, and you feel a constant need for the approval and acceptance of others. You don't like talking about yourself at all, and you are afraid of letting go. You refuse to make an effort to develop intimate relationships.

You're a worrier, who gets depressed easily. You run a minimum of risks. You're probably introverted, and find it very difficult to communicate. Other people see you as a loner, a bit of an outsider and, since you appear to care so little about your image, as someone who is lonely by choice. In reality, it is your fear of rejection that has condemned you to solitude.

If you scored between 20 and 50 points:

Your self-image does not quite correspond to the person you'd like to be. By trying to project an ideal image, you err on the side of excess, in order to mask your insecurity.

You want to make others believe that you are an exceptional being. And you end up believing it yourself. You're convinced that you're always right, and you're incapable of respecting other people's points of view.

You take criticism badly, and you have a strong tendency to treat others as inferior, an attitude which is not particularly conducive to forming lasting friendships. Everyone possesses some good qualities — you are certainly not the only one!

If you create an impression of being accessible to others, it's because you want to prove your own superiority. Therefore, instead of having a magnetic personality, you seem to alienate well-balanced people, who probably find you somewhat hard to take. On the other hand, you seem to attract persons of a submissive nature, who are easily depressed, and who lack self-confidence.

If you scored more than 50 points:
You have a good self-image, which probably corresponds pretty closely to reality. You seem to accept yourself the way you are, and you doubtless try to exploit your abilities to their fullest. You're a balanced person who respects other people. You're also a tolerant person. You attract friendship with ease, and people tend to put themselves out on your behalf. You're probably one of the small minority of persons who feel good about themselves.

You have no trouble attaining the goals you set for yourself. Continue as you are — you've discovered one of the secrets of happiness.

HOW TO IMPROVE YOUR IMAGE

You're going to change yourself completely — mentally, emotionally and physically!

How Do You See Yourself?

EXERCISE: FREE YOURSELF FROM THE PAST!

1. Get comfortable. Try to arrange not to be disturbed. Have a pen and some paper to hand. Your negative self-image is the result of precise causes, which go way back to your past. Write down the things you don't like about yourself, as well as the reasons you use to blame yourself for being the way you are. (For example: you find your physical appearance displeasing; overeating has caused you to gain weight; your moodiness has disrupted your marriage; you don't like your job, but you don't have the courage to quit and go back to school, and so on.)
2. Take your time — you may need a few days to run through your past and find out what's bothering you. Dig deep, and include even minor details. You'll be the only one ever to read this list, so don't be afraid to include things that you'd never admit to anyone else, even under torture!
3. When your list is complete, read it through, saying: 'I forgive myself, I'm cleaning the slate. Everyone has weaknesses — I'm not going to let mine destroy my sense of personal worth. I'm starting a new relationship with myself. And I have a new self-image — I respect myself the way I am.'
4. Take a match or a lighter, and ceremonially burn your list. If you don't like to play with fire, you can tear it up into a thousand pieces. Do this as a symbolic gesture. You've turned the page on your past.

Let's move on to the next exercise.

We're all a collection of habits. Our attitudes, emotions and gestures have, over the years, become habitual and routine. We've learned that to think or act in such and such a way in a given situation is correct and acceptable.

To change your personality and improve your self-image, you have to get rid of these habits. You do this simply by making conscious decisions. This exercise will help you modify your habitual modes of thinking and behaviour.

EXERCISE: REPROGRAMMING

1. Most people repeat the same series of activities every morning when they wake up: get out of bed, go to the bathroom, wash, get dressed, have breakfast. For the next two weeks, try reversing the order of two of these activities. For example, if you usually get dressed before having breakfast, do the reverse for the next two weeks, and so on.
2. That's not all: as you're carrying out these activities in their reverse order, think: 'I'm starting this day in a new way.' Then make a conscious decision that during the course of the day you're going to react differently from usual. For example, tell yourself:

    'Today I'm going to stay calm, whatever happens.'
    or:
    'Today I'm not going to criticize anyone.'
    or:
    'Today I'm going to eliminate all negative thoughts from my mind.'
    or simply:
    'Today I'm going to be as happy as possible.'
3. Each night think about the day that's passed and observe your attitudes. Were you able to attain the goal you set yourself that morning? If so, keep on. If not, start again. After two weeks, you'll feel like you've been given a new lease of life.

Does this exercise seem too simple? Well, as you'll soon see, it isn't as easy as all that to make a resolution in the morning and stick to it all day. Try it and see for yourself.

Changing your self-image does not mean developing an inflated ego. On the contrary, what you're trying to do is change your mental image, your own evaluation of yourself — in other words, the concept you have of your ego. It means recognizing and then modifying the erroneous and undervalued image you have of yourself.

You must understand this distinction if you want to go further with this method for success in life. If you have any doubts, read this chapter and the preceding one again, until it becomes clear.

SUMMARY

This chapter is especially important because it deals with the way we believe we are, our self-image.

The image you have of yourself affects your behaviour. If you see yourself as ugly, you will be ugly. If you see yourself as funny, you will be funny. And if your self-image is of an inferior person, then others will treat you as an inferior.

To gain people's friendship and support, to get people to find you interesting and balanced, your self-image has to project an interesting and balanced personality. If you don't like yourself, how can you expect others to like you?

By doing a simple test, you discovered how you actually see yourself. You then learned two exercises designed to help you remake your self-image, by exorcising what you don't like about yourself, and replacing these traits with positive resolutions for the future.

If you do the work required, two weeks should be enough time to lift the veils that have been hiding the 'real' you.

CHAPTER THREE

How to Develop Your Self-Confidence

THE MARVELS OF CONFIDENCE

Confidence is, first and foremost, the reflection of a positive self-image. To have confidence in yourself, you have to like yourself. To inspire confidence in others, you have to learn to have confidence in yourself.

To convince others, you first have to be convinced yourself. Why do charismatic people have absolutely no trouble finding people to rally behind them? Because they are already convinced that what they're doing is right.

By learning to appreciate yourself, by adopting the attitude that success will come to you as your right, since you are just as intelligent, competent and careful as anyone else, you increase your potential for success astronomically.

Self-confidence, however, is extremely volatile. It comes and goes without our knowing exactly why, at first glance.

Note that I said 'at first glance'. Why?

Because a few minutes of introspection is usually enough to resolve the mystery of why your self-confidence suddenly disappears.

CONFIDENCE BREEDS SUCCESS

When you were in school, you probably shared some of your apprehensions about exams with your parents, and they probably said something like, 'Well, if you don't think you can do it, then you won't be able to do it!' Or something along those lines.

As simple as it sounds, this principle should stay with us throughout our lives, like a guardian angel. Because confidence breeds success which, in turn, breeds more success. Lose your confidence, and you will experience failure after failure.

To acquire self-confidence, the kind that radiates from magnetic personalities and is a basic ingredient of charisma, you have to persevere. But it's not as difficult as you may think.

For example, do you remember the first time you rode a bicycle, or the first time you put on a pair of skates or skis? You were probably shaking with fear, like most people do. Yet today, riding a bike, skating or skiing seem like the most natural things in the world.

Do you remember when you were learning to drive? After finally mastering the arcane mystery of moving forward smoothly out of first gear — with gritted teeth and sweat pouring off your brow — you learned to manoeuvre in traffic, park, start facing up a hill, and so forth. Yet today you drive almost mechanically, without any trouble at all! You have complete confidence in your ability as a driver, and your success comes automatically.

HOW TO ACQUIRE THE CONFIDENCE YOU LACK

You are going to follow a progressive method which consists of two phases, each of those being subdivided into numerous steps.

First, you'll learn how to recognize your own worth and remain aware of it. Then comes learning how to affirm yourself, i.e. the practical application in day-to-day life of your newly acquired confidence.

PHASE 1: RECOGNIZE YOUR PERSONAL WORTH

Step one: build a file of your successes

Methodically enumerate your strong points, as well as the occasions on which you've put them to good use. Here are a few questions which may guide you in case you get stuck:

- In which areas do you possess special abilities? They may be professional abilities, or hobbies, sports, etc.
- What tangible things have you accomplished (academic or professional success, educating your children, success in your marriage or personal life, in sports, and so on)?
- On which occasions have you experienced the pleasure of success? Search through your memory, going back as far as you can — right to your childhood.
- What do people you know appreciate about you?

And so on. Don't underestimate yourself. In terms of self-confidence, it's just as important to know how to collect stamps as it is to change a spark plug in your car, or maintain a happy household.

Read and reread your list of successes. Keep it with you, and add to the list from time to time. Savour it, and impregnate your mind with the positive image it portrays, because that positive image is you!

Step two: be optimistic

We all fail at some time or other. Even the most charismatic people will sometimes fail in their endeavours. But unlike such persons, our reactions to failure can be catastrophic.

Many people brood over setbacks and disappointments, and finally allow them to dominate their entire lives! Are you one of those people?

If so, you have to change!

Confident people count their successes and not their failures. They forget the past and concentrate on the present and, of course, on the future. All their words and actions are illuminated by the light of optimism.

Now here's a little test which will help you determine whether you have a tendency towards optimism or pessimism. If you answer the questions honestly, you'll really be able to put your finger on the single most important concrete manifestation of your lack of self-confidence.

How to Develop Your Self-Confidence

TEST: ARE YOU AN OPTIMIST OR A PESSIMIST?

1 Someone places a glass containing water, wine, juice or any other drink you like in front of you. The glass is half filled. Your first thought is:
   a) *This glass is half empty*
   b) *This glass is half full.*

2 You pass a beautiful house, one that comes very close to being the house of your dreams. The first thing you think is:
   a) *I'll never be able to afford a house like that*
   b) *I hope the people living there appreciate their good fortune.*

3 You learn that someone at work is going to be promoted, but you don't know who. The first thing that comes to your mind is:
   a) *Well, in any case it won't be me*
   b) *There's a chance it could be me*

4 Before going out this morning, you noticed that the sky was overcast:
   a) *You take your raincoat and umbrella along, just' in case*
   b) *You tell yourself that it will most probably clear up as the day goes on.*

5 You're waiting for someone at the train station. The train arrives, but your friend isn't there. Your first thought is:
   a) *He (or she) must have had an accident on the way to the station*
   b) *He must have missed his train. I'll call his home in case he left a message and wants me to wait for the next one.*

Results

1 If you chose **b** for all the questions, then you know all about being an optimist. You're like a ray of sunshine to those around you. Everyone appreciates your optimistic attitude, and many people probably envy you for it. Don't change! You've found one of the keys to happiness, health, wisdom,

2   If you gave **a** answers to three, four or five questions, then it's high time you took a good look around you. Your life is probably dull and disorganised. You're a defeatist, a pessimist, and you're totally lacking in self-confidence. You worry over nothing. And you're probably one of those people whom everybody else finds a little depressing.

3   If you chose an **a** answer to one or two questions, then you're on the right track, but you still have some progress to make. It isn't possible to get rid of a pessimistic attitude that you've been carrying around your whole life in just a few days. However, if you do your part, you'll soon realize that it doesn't take much to tip the scales in favour of an optimistic approach. In a few weeks you should notice a significant improvement.

Do the following exercise for eight weeks:

EXERCISE: SELF-ANALYSIS

1   Get a notebook and a pen and take them with you wherever you go.

2   For the first two weeks, every time a negative thought enters your mind (like 'I'm sure to catch a cold in this weather...' or 'I know the heating is going to break down as soon as it gets cold...' or 'I know I'm going to ruin the casserole because we've got guests coming...') write it down in your notebook, next to the date on which it occurs.

Note: You'll probably notice that, as you approach the end of the first two-week period, you find yourself making many more entries than at first. Don't worry. It isn't because your state of mind is deteriorating, but simply because, as you get into the habit of writing down your negative thoughts, you become more aware of them, and fewer escape detection. The process of self-analysis is working!

3   For the next two weeks, ignore your negative thoughts. Concentrate exclusively on your positive thoughts, and write them down in your notebook under the appropriate date (things like, 'The weather's so beautiful, I'll be able to work in the garden this weekend . . .' or 'I think my new coat looks great on me . . .' etc.).

4   When these two weeks are over, sit down somewhere quiet and take a look at your notebook. Count your negative thoughts, and then your positive thoughts. In principle, an indication that your state of mind needs brightening up is that there are more entries on the negative side than on the positive.

5   Now look at each of your negative thoughts, and one by one replace them with a positive one. For example, if you wrote:
'What a drag, it's raining today. I won't be able to play tennis.'
you can replace this negative thought with something like:
'Well, it's raining! I'll be able to try out my new raincoat.'
or
'It's raining — great! The garden really needed it!'
or
'Raining? A perfect day for cleaning up my stamp collection.'

6   The following week, start all over again. Keep at it for at least two months. If you've been honest with yourself and made a real effort to write down your thoughts, the difference between the number of positive and negative thoughts should diminish. At some point, you'll start having more positive thoughts than negative ones. And a few days later, you'll realize that your negative thoughts have all but disappeared.

In this way you will eliminate the fears and doubts that are undermining your self-confidence, and are making you worry about events that never actually happen.

This exercise is essential to your success.

Stop reading and start the exercise right away. (If, for example, you don't believe the exercise will work, write down any doubts that come to mind.)

Step three: changing your attitude towards failure

The English language is equipped with numerous sayings, which are the fruit of popular experience. Here are two that you should always keep in mind:

'No risk, no gain.'

'Fortune smiles on the courageous.' (Fortune here refers to 'luck'.)

Actually, failure can only happen to someone who takes risks, who dares to try. If you've faced failure, it means that you dared to act, that you ran a risk, and that you possess the quality of initiative!

It's also only by trying that you succeed. So put yourself on the line, accept the risks, and you'll soon see the Goddess of Luck smiling down on you from above.

Consider whatever you undertake as a game. You lose some and you win some — no failure can diminish one iota of your worth as a person. On the contrary, it proves that you tried, that you showed courage and initiative, that you were dynamic.

Step four: stop seeing failure everywhere

How can a person see failure when it isn't there? You'll soon see.

EXERCISE: SORT AND FILE YOUR FAILURES

1   It's time to clean out your failure file. You're going to make a list of your personal, professional, athletic and social failures.

2   When the list is complete, analyse each of your failures individually. It's very probable that in nine out of ten cases:

- what you consider to have been YOUR failure was totally beyond your control — it had nothing to do with you at all;
- what you consider to be a failure wasn't really a failure, but simply dissatisfaction.

For example, some people feel badly about having failed their children by not encouraging them enough to get a good education, because these children would rather spend time out on the beach windsurfing than going to college. If you're one of those parents, then you'd better realize that your child's life belongs to him (or her), and that he's free to do what he wants. If he's happier windsurfing than calculating logarithms, that's his business. And you are not responsible! You did everything you could to make your children happy and well balanced. That's all your role as a parent requires.

3   When you've dissected the list of your failures, calmly and slowly tear it up into a thousand pieces. Do it as a kind of ceremony, as if you were performing an extremely important symbolic ritual. Afterwards, you should experience a sense of rebirth — you have been purified.

PHASE 2: AFFIRM YOURSELF

Now that you are convinced of your own personal worth, now that you've stopped underestimating yourself and envisage the future with a sense of growing optimism, it's a good idea to start applying your new self-image to everyday situations. Self-affirmation requires two fundamental abilities:

Knowing how to refuse
Knowing how to ask

Step one: learn how to say NO!
Why are we afraid to say no?

We run into people all our lives who try to boss us around and manipulate us, who try to get something from us or use us, or who simply try to dominate us completely, both psychologically and physically. It's up to us to make these people understand that we are in control of our own vital space, of our mental and emotional integrity, our free time, our money, and so on.

Have you ever found yourself saying 'yes' when you wanted to say no? Be honest. Most of us are afraid of saying no.

Why?

Fear of rejection
Psychologists attribute this reflex to a fear of being rejected. We think that if we refuse someone we will suffer disastrous consequences, the least of which is losing that person's friendship or affection.

Well, that may be true, you say, but when you buy a pair of shoes or a life insurance policy because the salesman or broker is relentless, is it still out of a fear of being rejected? After all, you hardly know the person!

Maybe so, but psychologists have discovered that most people can't stand being rejected by anyone, even by people they don't like or don't know. Interesting, isn't it?

People who never say no are also ashamed of being considered (horror of horrors!) selfish — if, for example, they dare refuse to entertain 25 guests for Christmas dinner, or refuse to be their children's chauffeur, or refuse to work overtime on a regular basis for no extra pay to please the boss.

What is the result of this attitude?

Are you accumulating resentment?
If you've never learned to say no, then you've certainly accumulated a toxic dose of resentment. You surely have the feeling you're being exploited, that you're the person everybody asks, because you always say yes . . .

Well, it's time to get rid of those toxins!

Charismatic people don't let anyone walk all over them. People like Napoleon, Roosevelt, Washington and Gandhi, to name just a few, were definitely not pushovers. It took a lot to convince them, and they certainly knew how to affirm themselves. Why not imitate them!

How to refuse
First, make sure to avoid all demonstrations of displeasure — sighs, shouts, tears, etc. Saying no doesn't mean you have to bring your fist crashing down on the table. What you do need to be is firm.

Five golden rules for saying no
Here are a few golden rules — you'll soon realize how effective they are.

1 Listen to the request attentively, and take time to think it over before answering. For example, if someone calls you up and asks you to go shopping with them, and you're not sure whether you feel like going, you could politely answer: 'I have to think about it. I'll call you back in a few minutes.'

2 Make sure you tell the truth. No lame excuses, no invented pretexts which you'll forget, no lies to make your life more complicated.

3 Get your message across tactfully and considerately. Refusing someone doesn't mean beating them to death. If you're asked to come to a meeting, for example, it would

be more diplomatic to say:

'Thanks for thinking about me, but I don't think I'll have the time.'

rather than:

'I don't want to go. It would be a complete waste of time for me.'

4. Don't make the mistake of arguing, especially when the other person gets aggressive. Stay calm and keep smiling. They are your best weapons against those who pretend to be shocked by your sudden refusal to comply with their wishes. Avoid getting into any kind of discussion about your refusal. You don't have to provide superfluous explanations. Just smile and say, 'No.'

   Let's look at an example: your spouse comes home from work and announces that he (or she) has invited a colleague over for dinner on Saturday night. He knows that you've been looking forward to going out on Saturday, to a movie or the theatre, and so he's going to try to get you to change your mind. If you really feel like going to the movie or the play, then there's no reason why you shouldn't go. Don't get involved in a long, drawn-out discussion, which could very well turn into a fight, during which both of you will probably say things you'll regret. Simply repeat, as politely and calmly as possible, your desire to go out on that night. Your spouse can entertain his guests on his own. 'Well,' I hear you saying, 'he's going to have to explain my absence somehow.' That's his problem, not yours.

5. Don't excuse yourself. There's no reason why you have to invent some excuse because you've said no to someone. It's your absolute right as an individual. By offering excuses, you place yourself in an inferior position, you reveal your fear and give the other person the impression that he can break through your defences and get you to change your mind. A discussion will follow, and you'll probably end up giving in just to have a little peace. Too bad!

How to Develop Your Self-Confidence

Here's some good news: according to specialists, the first 'no' is the most difficult. When you realize that this first refusal has not resulted in any cataclysmic disaster, then it becomes easier to refuse a second time. So what are you waiting for?

Step two: learn to ask
Why do you have to ask?

Because affirming yourself requires more than negative responses. Affirming yourself also means knowing how to ask for things. Another proverb will illustrate the point: 'Giving is sweeter than receiving.'

Everybody likes to give. It inflates the ego, it makes us feel worthy, it creates a deep feeling of satisfaction in us. But if you don't ask for anything, you risk being overlooked.

Other people can't always guess what you expect of them. And in fact they are under no obligation to try to figure out what you want. Even your spouse, your parents and your closest friends cannot know exactly what's going on inside your head at the precise moment you desire something.

Do you want to have a party on your birthday? Let people know about it. Your friends and family will be only too glad to organize a little surprise for you! On the other hand, if you keep telling everyone that birthdays really don't mean anything to you, that you've stopped counting, and so on, then don't be surprised if your spouse forgets to give you a present!

Let's imagine that a job opens up at work that you're very interested in. Don't wait until it's offered to you. Go and talk to your superior and let him/her know what you want. Explain how you would handle the job, and why you think you're especially qualified.

Perhaps self-sacrifice and modesty are Christian virtues, but you can be sure that they never gave Napoleon a crown, or Ronald Reagan two terms in the White House, or made Bill Cosby the wealthiest performer in history!

What demands do you find most difficult to make?
Think about your family, social, professional and sexual life, etc,

and decide which demands you find most difficult to make. Number them according to degree of difficulty, starting with the most difficult.

Now practise formulating these demands, starting with the easiest and working up to the hardest, in the first person ('I . . .'.) First write them down, and then read them over from time to time.

Learn to take
Once you've obtained what you want, the moment arrives when you have to accept it graciously.

You must recall how certain people reacted when you had the pleasure of giving them a beautiful present: 'Oh, you're crazy! You shouldn't have spent so much money! I really didn't need this . . .'

What could be more depressing?

Not only do you feel ridiculous and hurt, you feel like an idiot for spending so much on something that won't even be appreciated, and that you can't take back.

Now take some time to examine your own conscience, and think about the times when you reacted this way to something someone gave you, or did for you.

You need as much generosity to take as to give
If someone makes an effort to give you something, or to do something for you, show how much you appreciate it. You'll make that person happy, he or she will want to do things for you again, and your esteem will grow by degrees.

SUMMARY

This method helps you discover what you can do to increase your self-confidence. After pinpointing the ingredients that confidence is made of, you drew up a list of your successes, which you now keep close at hand, periodically making additions.

You learned how important the element of optimism is to a charismatic personality. If you feel you have certain tendencies towards being pessimistic, correct them right away. You'll be happier, healthier, and more charismatic.

Also, you know that acquiring the magnetic personality you dream of having requires knowing how to affirm yourself. And affirming yourself is primarily a question of knowing how to say no.

You are now aware of why it is so difficult to say no: fear of being rejected or of appearing to be selfish. There are ways to say no without hurting anyone — you have to be diplomatic and sensitive, while remaining firm and concise.

But self-affirmation also has its positive side: you also have to learn how to ask for things. No one can guess exactly what's going on in your mind. Don't wait for others to try and figure out what you want. Ask, and you will receive.

CHAPTER FOUR

How to Overcome Your Shyness and Develop Your Courage

How often have you found yourself trembling, heart pounding, legs weak, cheeks on fire, when facing a colleague or your boss, a teacher or a traffic cop, or simply a person of the opposite sex?

Shyness can be paralysing at any age. It causes bizarre anxieties, nightmares, indigestion and, when the occasion to be strong and affirmative has passed, infinite regrets.

Do you think you're beyond hope?

If you do, you're wrong. Shyness can be treated. You might not be aware that most psychologists who have published works on the subject were at one time very shy themselves. Who is more likely to be interested in shyness, and write hundreds of pages about it, than a person who is shy!

Those who have never suffered from shyness are incapable of understanding the extent to which it can ruin our lives and make us unhappy.

Self-assurance, confidence and ease of expression are the main qualities of a magnetic personality. If being shy is forcing you to hide behind a shell, then you're missing out on many of the beauties of existence. Throw away your shell, and learn to live a full and satisfying life!

TEST: WHAT KIND OF SHY PERSON ARE YOU?

This is no joke. There are varying degrees and numerous types of shyness. This test will tell you what category you belong to.

How to Overcome Your Shyness and Develop Your Courage

1. You're invited to a party with 30 other people. You only know one of them:
   a) *You don't leave that person's side the whole evening*
   b) *You chat with two or three other people, who seem as alone as you are*
   c) *You move from one group to another, and take advantage of the opportunity to make new acquaintances.*

2. You have to go to an interview for a new job:
   a) *You don't sleep the night before*
   b) *You have a hard time getting to sleep, convinced that the other candidates have more chance of getting the job than you do*
   c) *You get a good night's sleep, confident of your abilities and qualifications.*

3. You arrive late for a conference, and realise that the entrance is right in front of the audience:
   a) *You walk right in*
   b) *You wait in the hallway for another latecomer, and slip in behind*
   c) *You wait for a break in the proceedings before entering.*

4. During a group discussion, you're asked to voice your opinion about a subject that is familiar to you:
   a) *You feel uncomfortable because people are looking at you, but you are able to provide an acceptable explanation*
   b) *You're taken by surprise, and find yourself incapable of expressing yourself coherently*
   c) *You provide a clear and concise explanation, without feeling in the least embarrassed.*

5. At a meeting where the participants are asked to state their views:
   a) *You never take the floor because you're convinced that you have nothing important to say*
   b) *You speak out whenever you have a suggestion*
   c) *You take the floor, and joke a bit before stating your opinion in a clear and concise manner.*

6. The opinions of your colleagues:
   a) *Sometimes cause you to change your attitude in order to please them*
   b) *Slide off you like water off a duck's back*
   c) *Often prevent you from sleeping.*

7. You're waiting in a queue when a few people push in front of you:
   a) *You automatically step back in front of them*
   b) *You ask them firmly but politely not to jump the queue*
   c) *You're afraid they'll get aggressive and don't say anything.*

8. You're discussing a subject you don't know much about with a group of specialists:
   a) *You are very impressed, and feel somewhat inadequate*
   b) *You avoid saying much because you're not familiar with the subject, but you don't feel inferior because you do have a lot of expertise in other fields*
   c) *You admit your ignorance, and show a desire to learn more*

9. You find yourself with a group of people who are somewhat snobbish:
   a) *You let them know that you're nobody's fool*
   b) *You try to be as snobbish as they are*
   c) *You're very impressed, and don't dare say anything for fear of appearing ridiculous.*

10. Your boss turns around and blames you for doing exactly what he asked you to do:
    a) *You start excusing yourself and feel guilty*
    b) *You excuse yourself and explain that you had trouble understanding his orders correctly*
    c) *You remind him of his orders, politely but firmly.*

11. You're in the waiting room of a doctor who specialises in sexually transmitted diseases:
    a) *You wonder what the other people must think of you*

b) *You behave as if you were in any other waiting room*
   c) *You try to let the other patients know that you haven't got that kind of problem.*

12 Do you wear sunglasses:
   a) *Never*
   b) *Sometimes*
   c) *Very often.*

13 When you have to make a speech or a presentation:
   a) *You concentrate only on what you're going to say, and neglect to listen to other people's speeches*
   b) *You half listen, but you're distracted*
   c) *You listen closely, and adapt your own speech to what has been said before.*

14 You get the impression that other people:
   a) *Treat you as an equal*
   b) *Treat you with condescension*
   c) *Make fun of you.*

15 When someone compliments you:
   a) *You feel uncomfortable, and mutter a few indistinct words in return*
   b) *You transfer the credit to someone else, and quickly change the subject*
   c) *You thank the person who complimented you.*

16 When someone says something nasty about you:
   a) *You are incapable of replying on the spot, and then spend the next two hours regretting that you didn't come up with this or that retort*
   b) *You feel rejected, misunderstood and disliked*
   c) *You reply immediately.*

17 Do you think that others know how shy you are?
   a) *Somewhat*

How to Develop Charisma & Personal Magnetism

    b) *Absolutely*
    c) *Not at all.*

18 When someone you don't know raises their voice nearby:
    a) *You immediately feel guilty*
    b) *You think that the person needs to learn more self-control*
    c) *You laugh about it because whatever the cause is, it doesn't concern you.*

19 You're on vacation, and someone invites you to join their group for dinner:
    a) *You refuse because you don't know the people, and end up eating alone*
    b) *You refuse at first, but then feel obligated to accept when the person insists*
    c) *You accept or decline, according to your mood, without feeling in the least disturbed.*

20 Your shyness:
    a) *Prevents you from saying what you think*
    b) *Makes you say things that you really don't think*
    c) *Does not prevent you from expressing yourself.*

Results

QUESTION	POINTS SCORED
1	a = 5 b = 3 c = 0
2	a = 5 b = 3 c = 0
3	a = 0 b = 3 c = 5
4	a = 3 b = 5 c = 0
5	a = 5 b = 0 c = 3
6	a = 3 b = 0 c = 5
7	a = 3 b = 0 c = 5
8	a = 5 b = 3 c = 0
9	a = 0 b = 3 c = 5
10	a = 5 b = 3 c = 0

How to Overcome Your Shyness and Develop Your Courage

Results

QUESTION	POINTS SCORED
11	a = 5 b = 0 c = 3
12	a = 0 b = 3 c = 5
13	a = 5 b = 3 c = 0
14	a = 0 b = 3 c = 5
15	a = 5 b = 3 c = 0
16	a = 3 b = 5 c = 0
17	a = 0 b = 5 c = 3
18	a = 5 b = 3 c = 0
19	a = 3 b = 5 c = 0
20	a = 5 b = 3 c = 0

If you scored between 70 and 100 points:
You are deeply and obsessively shy. You probably gave up trying to overcome your shyness, which has ruined your life and prevented you from fulfilling yourself, a long time ago. Other people probably find you nice, if a little stand-offish. When you're with people you don't know, you hide your shyness by being distant, which unfortunately comes across as arrogance.

If you scored between 40 and 70 points:
You are shy, certainly, but you often succeed in hiding it. You're very self-conscious, and make constant efforts to express yourself and gain other people's respect. This usually works, and people who don't know you well are fooled. You must have a whole series of little 'tricks' that create the illusion of self-assurance and courage. You're a person who hides your shyness.

If you scored less than 40 points:
You suffer from occasional bouts of shyness, but they're not frequent enough to affect your life, and you've learned to make the effort required to overcome attacks of shyness that could cause problems. You may have become more self-assured as you

matured. Or maybe your successes have improved your self-image and given you the confidence you lacked. Or you may just feel comfortable doing exactly what you like. Whatever the reason, you are only occasionally and slightly shy.

STEP 1: IDENTIFY YOUR ENEMY

To fight an enemy, you first have to know who or what it is. Therefore, the aim of the first exercise is to study your shyness objectively. Over the next few days, you're going to observe your shyness in action, coldly and clinically, as if you were a specialist examining an interesting prehistoric specimen which everyone thought had been extinct for hundreds of thousands of years.

EXERCISE: SPLIT YOUR PERSONALITY

1. Get comfortable in front of a mirror and look at yourself attentively. The person you see is a stranger whom you're meeting for the first time. Observe yourself curiously. Absorb the image in front of you. You should always keep it in mind.

2. From now on you will be split into two persons: an 'actor' who goes through the movements of day-to-day living, and an 'observer' who stands in the wings and carefully examines those acts and gestures. Try to see yourself, exactly as you did in the mirror. Never lose sight of yourself!

3. Get a notebook and pen, and keep them with you constantly for the next two weeks.

4. For two weeks, observe yourself getting up in the morning, taking a shower, getting dressed, eating breakfast and

leaving for work. Watch yourself walking in the street, taking the bus, shopping, etc.

5 At some point during the day, you're going to confront your shyness. But not right away. Take time to observe yourself carrying out mundane and familiar activities, which don't require any special effort. After a few hours, the mechanism of splitting and observing yourself will come naturally. And that's when you will be asked to do something that will force you to take charge of yourself. It could concern a meeting with your boss, or a request you have to make from someone you don't know, or trying to get a refund from a supplier, etc.

6 Every time you feel an attack of shyness coming on, do what is called a 'stop-frame' in movie jargon. Immediately ask yourself the following questions and write your answers down in your notebook.

What am I afraid of at this moment? That the person I have to deal with will find me ridiculous? Or that I'm not dressed well enough? Or that my make-up ran because I had to walk in the rain? That they'll be aggressive? That my boss is calling me into his office to criticize my work? Maybe that what I'm wearing makes him uncomfortable? And so on.

If you're really shy, you'll have no trouble identifying these types of questions and answering them straightaway, because the situation is familiar to you. However, this will be the first time you analyse your behaviour objectively.

7 Each night, take a few minutes to study the answers you hastily scrawled in your notebook. Transform passive thoughts ('What do you want from me? I'm shy! It isn't my fault . . .') to active ones ('I am shy, but I'm doing something about it . . .')

8 Find a remedy for each reason you wrote down for your shyness. For example:
'I felt intimidated because I was afraid my boss would

criticize me. But why should he have any reason to criticize me? Did I make a mistake? If so, how can I rectify it?'
'I don't like walking down this corridor because it's always full of people, sitting around and watching what's going on. So what? Should I be ashamed of the way I look? Of my clothes, of my hair? Why? What concrete steps can I take so that I won't be ashamed of myself any more? What if it's all in my head? What if everyone isn't looking at me?'

The four main causes of shyness

If you apply yourself, it shouldn't take more than two weeks to determine the causes of your shyness, and the kinds of situations that set off your fear reflex. Don't worry, there aren't that many! In general, shyness is caused by:

- shame of our physical appearance, either of our body or our clothes;
- fear of aggression from unknown persons, either mocking or scornful;
- fear of being rejected by persons we consider important (both in our private and professional lives);
- a feeling of superiority (oh yes!) which causes us to imprison ourselves in an 'ivory tower'.

After two weeks of doing this exercise you'll notice that your powers of observation are considerably sharpened. You'll find yourself reacting differently to situations that you find terrifying, or that make you uncomfortable. You'll feel that you've already made some progress, without knowing exactly where the improvement lies.

How to attack the root of the problem

Actually, what has happened is that you've taken the 'drama' out of your shyness. It's very difficult to get upset about a situation that you're able to analyse objectively.

As long as your shyness remained some kind of omnipresent but vague enemy, a mysterious, frightening dragon that reared its ugly head out of the depths of your imagination from time to time, it was terrifying. But as soon as you're able to put your finger on the essential root of the problem, by objectively answering the questions you've learned to ask yourself, you've already covered a good deal of ground on the road to victory.

You're not completely cured, of course! The shyness you've been carrying around for 10, 20 or even 30 years is not going to disappear in two weeks. You are still shy, and you may always be a little shy.

Understanding others better

An important element of the path you've just taken is the lucidity which it has automatically given you. The role of observer, which you've been playing for the past few weeks, has allowed you not only to identify your own motivations, but also to gain some insight into the motivations of others.

There's no mystery involved.

By sharpening your perception of yourself, you also get rid of the apprehension which has prevented you from seeing others as they are, in the full light of day. Where before you saw some kind of ogre, you now see an ordinary human being. So a person who seemed arrogant and frightening now appears insecure, hiding their feelings of inferiority behind an aggressive personality, full of sabre-rattling bravado and boasting.

You'll need a few more weeks of discipline, as well as a reasonable dose of introspection and honesty. But you've already passed the most difficult part of the test — you are now able to confront your shyness.

Even if you remain somewhat reserved and uncomfortable in the limelight for the rest of your life, don't worry. Being a little shy is not a defect — on the contrary, most of us are put off by people who are too arrogant, too sure of themselves, who impose themselves on others without ever considering that they might not be appreciated. Modesty, tact and sensitivity are all qualities that should be cultivated.

STEP 2: BALANCE THE ACCOUNTS

The time has come to balance the accounts on your two weeks of 'split personality' observations.

Get comfortable, with your notebook handy, and ask yourself these questions:

- Do you feel you know yourself better?
- Do you think you have more control over your imagination?
- Have your faculties of observation improved?
- Do you laugh more often?
- Have you noticed that you're less likely to be clumsy in your day-to-day activities?
- Do you think you've got to the root of your shyness?
- Do you feel as frightened as before by other people?

Logically, you should observe a significant improvement.

Now the next question is very important. If you can honestly answer in the affirmative, then you're doing very well. If not, you should continue with the 'split personality' exercise — go back to the beginning and start all over again.

- Do you have a greater understanding of what motivates other people?

STEP 3: ELIMINATE NEGATIVE IMAGES

The preceding method was designed to help you confront your shyness head on, and to analyse it from a number of different points of view. It was a general method. Why not add a few more exercises, which are more precise and designed to overcome certain specific aspects of your shyness? You have nothing to lose, and everything to gain!

You're probably convinced that being shy makes you some kind of inferior being. To fight this negative image you have of yourself, open your faithful notebook and do the following exercise:

EXERCISE: COST – BENEFIT

In this exercise, you're going to make a list of the advantages and disadvantages of the negative image you have of yourself. You're convinced that your shyness is detrimental to your value as a person. This conviction has advantages and disadvantages.

You're going to write them down clearly, in black and white, in two columns, and then calculate the percentage of advantages as opposed to disadvantages.

Then you'll do exactly the same thing, only using a positive self-image as a base, something like: 'My shyness doesn't make me an inferior being – I'm just human, vulnerable and sensitive.'

Here's an example of some of the things you could write down in this excellent exercise:

Negative idea: My shyness reduces my value as a person

Advantages of this conviction:
1 This attitude forces me to master my feelings and hide my weaknesses.
2 If I hide my feelings well, people won't realize just how badly I feel about myself, and won't reject me.

33%

Disadvantages of this conviction:
1 Trying to hide my true self only emphasizes my shyness.
2 My shyness creates the impression that nothing about me is positive, and that I'm incapable of doing anything.
3 My self-esteem is zero.
4 I am lonely, because I can't share my feelings with other people.

67%

Positive image: My shyness is just part of being human — I'm vulnerable and sensitive like everyone else

1. I can stop hating myself because I have no reason to doubt my self-worth.
2. I now know that I can cure my shyness. I am fully capable of doing it.
3. I'll be less afraid to talk to other people, because there's absolutely no reason why they should think I'm stupid or a failure.

75%

Disadvantages of this image:
1. By taking my chances with other people, I risk being rejected.

25%

Here again, clarity and objectivity are your best allies.

By coldly analyzing the advantages and disadvantages of the image you have of yourself, you can exorcise the demon that has been haunting you for so long. But I must repeat that complete honesty is essential if you hope to succeed.

Now it's your turn.

EXERCISE: INNER DIALOGUE

This exercise is also designed to help you combat your ingrained negative self-image. You'll be making use of the split personality technique once again, since you'll be asking the questions as well as supplying the answers.

1. Each day, write down three negative thoughts which make you shy.
2. Next, find positive thoughts to counterbalance these negative ideas.
3. Keep doing this for two weeks.

How to Overcome Your Shyness and Develop Your Courage

The following are some examples of the kind of inner dialogue you should be having. You shouldn't have any trouble using them as a model for identifying your own anxieties:

Negative idea:
'I'm very attracted to this person, but I don't think it's the right place to start a conversation.'
Positive idea:
'If I feel like talking to someone, the place has nothing to do with it.'

Negative idea:
'I don't dare walk down this hallway because it's always full of people.'
Positive idea:
'I must be pretty self-centred if I think that these people have nothing better to do than watch me and criticize me.'

Negative idea:
'It shouldn't be an effort to make friends. It should happen naturally, by itself.'
Positive idea:
'In life, nothing happens on its own. There's nothing wrong with making an effort to meet people and forge lasting friendships.'

Negative idea:
'If I talk to someone I don't know, they'll immediately think I'm out to get something.'
Positive idea:
'If he or she is incapable of differentiating between friendly conversation and some kind of underhand proposition, that's their problem, not mine.'

STEP 4: YOU'RE NOT ALONE!

Shy people are often arrogant.

'What!' I hear you say, 'isn't that a contradiction in terms?'

Well, you read correctly. Shy people are arrogant because they imagine — and this is one of the underlying causes of shyness — that they're unique, that they're one of a kind, that no one else on earth is as shy as they are.

If that's not arrogance, then what is?

You're wrong to believe that you're the only shy person on earth, that no one else suddenly finds themselves with a dry mouth and pounding heart and butterflies in their stomach when facing a person of authority.

To convince yourself, do the following 'survey' exercise.

EXERCISE: SURVEY

This exercise will expand your horizons considerably.

As its name indicates, you're going to conduct a survey amongst your friends and acquaintances. Tell them you're interested in the subject, and that you'd appreciate it if they helped with your survey on shyness.

Copy the following survey questionnaire and ask as many people as you can to write down their responses, instructing them to answer as honestly as possible.

You are free to add any questions that come to mind, adapting them to your subjects.

Survey

1. Have you ever felt nervous when talking to a person of the opposite sex for the first time?

2. Do you have to make an effort to invite someone you find attractive to go out with you?

3. Do you feel nervous and anxious when you have to speak in public?

4. In what type of normal situations do you feel most shy or uncomfortable?

5 Do you suffer from any physical symptoms when you have to take an oral exam or be interviewed for a job?

6 Do you think that shy people are inferior?

What conclusions can you draw from the exercise?
This exercise will prove that a large number of people, even those who seem most self-assured, have at one time or another in their lives felt the same symptoms of shyness as you. This discovery should reassure you, and eradicate that terrible feeling of solitude which often troubles shy people.

From now on, the fact of knowing that you're not alone will represent a large step on your path towards overcoming your shyness altogether.

Others feel no more at ease than you

Think back to the days when you were just a young student at school. Didn't you ever get to school in the morning with your homework unfinished because you weren't able to find the answer to some maths or physics problem? Your heart was probably pounding with anxiety. You timidly started asking your fellow students if they had managed to find the answer.

To your great relief, you discovered that the other kids were also stuck on the problem. No one was able to come up with the solution. 'Wow, I'm not the only one!' you thought, and your anxieties instantly disappeared.

This is exactly what will happen to you when you realise firsthand that you're not the only person on earth suffering from shyness.

Do your exercises every day for at least six months, in stages of two weeks at a time. You'll realize that your shyness is gradually diminishing, allowing other people to feel more comfortable with you. This will be a double victory, since both you and everyone you come into contact with will benefit!

Improve your social skills

A last piece of advice to help you fight your shyness towards other people: read a book about improving your social skills.

This is no joke.

Although many of these books are outdated and refer to a lifestyle that has long since become obsolete, some of the more modern ones contain a quantity of useful advice on what attitudes to adopt and how to behave in the company of others. They provide clear answers to questions we ask ourselves all the time, but don't dare ask others, for fear of appearing ignorant or naive.

A great sense of security

You don't have to follow these authors' advice to the letter. Use your common sense. But you'll quickly realize that the simple fact of knowing exactly what should and should not be done in a given situation — what is acceptable and what isn't — will give you a great feeling of security. Because when you're with company, shyness is often provoked or exacerbated by your ignorance of accepted forms of social behaviour, i.e. by your fear of doing something stupid and appearing clumsy and uneducated.

Get rid of this aspect of shyness! It's easy to eliminate, so why not do it. Find out exactly how you should behave in your day-to-day encounters. You'll soon acquire a degree of self-assurance that will astonish you!

SUMMARY

The shyness that has ruined your life up to now is not an invicible enemy. It's not even as powerful a force as you thought.

The extremely simple method you learned in this chapter is based on three principles. The first consists of getting you to analyse objectively your shyness and negative thoughts about yourself. This enables you to see the enemy for what it really is.

Next you combat the acquired ideas that are often the root

cause of shyness. By analyzing the advantages and disadvantages of these acquired ideas, you'll realize that it's much more profitable to get rid of them than to drag them around with you, like weights chained to your ankles.

You're not the only person on earth to feel unpleasant physical and psychological symptoms when confronted with certain situations. On the contrary — everybody does to some extent. Join the human race, and stop hiding in your ivory tower of shyness.

Finally, read a book on social etiquette. It will provide you with a marvellous feeling of security. There's nothing like knowing exactly the 'right thing' to do or say to instil a sense of self-assurance in yourself!

CHAPTER FIVE

Improve Your Physical Appearance

Our physical appearance is the first thing people see, and is the way we introduce ourselves to the world outside. Long before becoming aware of our qualities and faults, people judge us based on the way we look.

Whether we like it or not, the way we look is a reflection of our inner life, because although we are not responsible for our inherited physical characteristics, we have unconsciously modified them during the course of our lives so that they are in accord with our personality.

If you feel uncomfortable with other people, if you're extremely shy, it's partly because you don't feel good about yourself. You find your physical appearance displeasing — something to be ashamed of.

By physical appearance I don't only mean the shape of your face or the cut of your hair, but also things like your voice, the way you look at people, your posture and bearing, the way you dress, and so on. If you don't feel good about yourself, it's because you don't like one or a number of these elements and you develop a complex about them.

You must get rid of these degrading feelings! As long as you don't, they will continue to hinder your progress and prevent you from reaching your full potential.

TEST: YOUR PHYSICAL WELL-BEING

To find out what kind of relationship you have with your body, do the following test, answering yes or no to each question.

Improve Your Physical Appearance

1. Do you look down at your feet when you walk?
2. Do you sometimes feel pain in your neck muscles?
3. Are you prone to muscular pain in the rest of your body (thighs, for example)?
4. Do you stoop, or do your shoulder blades protrude?
5. When you talk to someone, do you look them in the eyes?
6. Do you have back problems?
7. Do you hesitate a lot when you talk?
8. Are you prone to dropping things that you're holding?
9. Do you make a lot of noise when you move things around?
10. Do you drag your feet when you walk?
11. Do you suffer from any nervous tics?
12. Are you constantly preoccupied with your weight?
13. Is your body overtly out of proportion (one shoulder higher than the other, one hip larger than the other, etc.)?
14. When you're seated, are you constantly changing the position of your legs?
15. If you were given the opportunity to change your body, would you immediately accept?

Results
Give yourself 1 point for each affirmative answer.

If you scored 5 points or less:
You don't need to read this chapter. You know yourself, you accept yourself, and you consider your body a friend. You are comfortable being who you are. If you suffer from shyness and lack confidence, it's not because you're ashamed of your body. You'll have to look elsewhere for the causes of your lack of self-assurance.

If you scored between 6 and 10 points:
Your energy isn't flowing freely to all parts of your body. These blockages are preventing you from expressing yourself and feeling good about yourself. You are making an effort to overcome the discomfort your body causes you, but you don't have a very good image of yourself. However, you're far from being a lost cause!

If you scored between 11 and 15 points:
The situation is serious. You're very probably one of those people who 'carry the weight of the world on their shoulders'. You may have an ungainly appearance, a shuffling walk, and your introverted nature is reflected by your posture and attitude. You probably hate your body, and have a disastrous image of yourself. You don't pay attention to the way you dress in order to enhance your appearance. You must start making an effort! Don't continue ruining your life in this way. The solution is easier than you think!

BODY LANGUAGE

You are aware that the body has its own language. You've known it since you were an adolescent, when just the way someone looked at you, or winked or smiled or walked, indicated that they were interested in making contact.

When we want to convince someone, we tend to make more use of our bodies — nodding the head, speaking quickly, gesturing with our hands and arms, etc.

When we're self-confident, we speak more slowly, with less exaggerated gestures. People of German, English or Scandinavian origin use gestures much less frequently when they speak. On the other hand, Latin people, as everyone knows, use gestures to accompany almost every word they utter.

If you are resisting an argument, you're likely to cross your arms. If you want to think something over, you'd touch your forehead, or bite your lip, or scratch your nose. Each one of us has our repertoire of mannerisms.

The body language of people we listen to willingly, people who are charismatic and draw others to them, betrays no tension, no nervousness or anxiety — just relaxation and quiet reflection. These people radiate an aura of serenity and calm. When they want to convince someone, they use simple, studied gestures and speak in a warm and usually deep voice.

Improve Your Physical Appearance

Our bodies are constantly talking. That's why, if you scored between 11 and 15 points on the previous test, the message your body is transmitting is that you don't feel good being yourself, that you don't like your appearance, and that you suffer from an acute sense of discomfort 24 hours a day. You're certainly not going to acquire the magnetic personality you desire if you continue sending messages like those!

Before discussing the fundamental modifications of your physical characteristics, let's look at what you could do to improve the general appearance of the person you see every time you glance in a mirror.

HOW TO IMPROVE YOUR 'LOOK'

Appearance is a collection of a number of equally important factors: posture, breathing, gestures, gait, voice and, of course, your gaze.

If you can't determine exactly what it is about your appearance that doesn't work, then do the following programme step by step — you won't regret it!

YOUR POSTURE

'Stand up straight! You look like a saxophone! You're going to get a hunchback!'

How many times did you hear these kinds of admonitions from parents and teachers when you were a child? At least once a day, I'm sure! Their praiseworthy intention was to prevent us from developing a deformed spine or hunched shoulders. But bad posture can have other consequences which are just as harmful.

If you've developed the habit of bad posture, energy cannot circulate properly to the various parts of your body, and the balance of your entire nervous system will suffer sooner or later.

Posture is also one of the aspects of non-verbal communication that you use when talking to other people. If you stand there rigidly, looking like someone who's just swallowed a broom, you're going to put the other person on the defensive. On the other hand, if you're slouched down on a chair or a couch, you may offend the other person by transmitting a message of indifference or even disdain.

Here are a few exercises essential for maintaining good posture:

How to create an impression of self confidence

Standing position
This position is very simple. Imagine that the crown of your skull is suspended from the ceiling by an invisible string, which stretches down through your spine and hips. Alternatively, imagine that you're balancing a ball on the top of your head.

Check the position of your legs — they should be straight without being stiff. When standing, your weight should be equally supported by both legs. Your feet should be flat on the ground. Relax your shoulders and arms. Imagine yourself anchored to the ground. If someone came along and pushed you accidentally, you should be able to maintain your balance.

Avoid positions that block energy circulation: shoulders raised, fists clenched, arms crossed, head bowed, your weight on one leg, etc.

Try checking your posture the next time you're waiting for the bus, or queuing at the cinema. If you're standing correctly, the wait will seem a lot shorter.

Sitting position
This is what matters most, since we spend most of our time sitting down.

How should we sit?

To start with, the chair shouldn't be too high or too low — thighs and shins should form a right angle, with the feet flat on

Improve Your Physical Appearance

the floor. If the chair has armrests, place your elbows on them, with your fingers resting on the end. If you want to change position, rest your arms lightly on your thighs.

And now for the back, your poor tortured, mistreated, unhappy back . . .

Your back should also be straight, forming a 90° angle with your thighs. To keep your back straight, you should be seated right up against the back of the chair, and not just perched on the front, as you probably often do . . . This is of critical importance! If you get tired, shift your hips forward a little and change the position of your spine for a while.

If you do perch on the edge of the chair, you're transmitting a message that you're tense or anxious, uncomfortable or intimidated. And this is in complete contradiction to the relaxed, confident image that you want to project, isn't it!

What makes a good chair?

Having a good chair is just as important as having a good mattress. If you work sitting down, equip yourself with a quality chair, adapted to your back and to the kind of work you do and the tools you use. If you spend your days writing by hand, you wouldn't want the same chair as someone who works on a computer or someone who does graphics.

There are very well designed, high-tech chairs on the market, called 'ergonomic' (a new discipline which studies the interface between man and machines), which offer excellent support for the body. Unfortunately, most of them cost a small fortune. If you work for a large company, suggest that they look into equipping the office with ergonomic furniture the next time they update their equipment. The investment might be worthwhile in terms of increased productivity. If you work for yourself, and can't afford the expense, try to pick one up second hand.

EXERCISE: IMPROVE YOUR POSTURE

Before starting the exercise itself, you'll have to find someone to help you. Give them a large felt pen or crayon (one that's easy to erase).

1. Like most people, you probably own a full-length mirror. If not (if you've refused to allow one in your house because you can't stand looking at yourself!), now's the time to get one. From now on you'll enjoy looking at yourself in the mirror!

2. Get down on all fours in front of the mirror. Your thighs form a right angle with your trunk on one side, and your arms form a right angle with your trunk on the other.

3. Ask your assistant to draw a straight horizontal line on the mirror a little above the line formed by your back (about 4 to 6 inches, for example).

4. Once a day, get back into the position described in paragraph 2 and stay that way for at least one minute. The line of your back should be perfectly parallel to the line drawn on the mirror. If it isn't, adjust it slowly, without making any sudden movements.

5. After staying in this position for a few seconds, you'll tend to curve or arch your back. Whenever this happens, rectify the position immediately.

If you do the exercise regularly, in just a few weeks you'll notice that your muscle pains have been eased significantly, your back is less curved, and you can stand up straight a lot easier.

EXERCISE FOR RELAXING THE SHOULDERS

This exercise is especially recommended for women, who have

Improve Your Physical Appearance

a tendency to hunch their shoulders to avoid overly exposing their breasts. But many men also have tightly hunched shoulders and will also benefit from the exercise, which is so simple a child can do it.

1. Remove your shoes and stand with your back against a wall, arms relaxed by your sides. Your heels should also be touching the wall.

2. Open your shoulders so that they too are touching the wall. Your chest will expand somewhat as you feel your shoulder blades touching the wall.

3. Count to 30, then relax your shoulder muscles.

4. Count to 10, then resume the position. Repeat the exercise at least 10 times.

2 THE WAY YOU WALK

If you're a woman, you may have found yourself staring enviously at those creatures who populate airports, offices and, of course, fashion salons, who seem to walk with an ethereal grace, their bodies in perfect harmony, their movements fluid and seemingly effortless, transmitting a message of total serenity.

If you're a man, you must, on occasion, have admired the way some young guy, walking beside you or across the road, seemed to exude a sense of relaxation and confidence, while you felt constricted and clumsy in comparison.

The way we walk says a lot about who we are. It can be hurried or dragging, jumpy or smooth, heavy or light, clumsy or confident, and so on.

So the message sent by your gait must be taken seriously!

EXERCISE: THE IDEAL WALK

The ideal walk is relaxed but not sloppy, neither too slow nor too fast. You use your whole body, not just your feet. Your whole leg should move, right up to the hip (unlike Charlie Chaplin and his famous shuffle!). Your shoulders should follow the movements of your hips. Your arms should swing effortlessly by your sides — just let them hang and move naturally.

1. Face your new friend (your own image in the full length mirror, of course!). Start by lifting one leg, feeling all the muscles you put into action. Place that foot on the floor and lift the other leg. Take your time and study your movements.

2. Feel all the movements of your body which come into play when you walk: arms, head, hips. Each time you lift a foot, move your entire leg — you should feel your hip moving.

3. Practise walking in front of the mirror for at least five minutes a day.

Note: Just as your posture can suffer from the type of chair you sit on to work (especially if it's of inferior quality), so your walk can become deformed if you don't wear the right kind of shoes. Short women especially tend to wear extremely high heels, which makes their walk heavy and graceless, and hurts their feet and heels, not to mention their spines. Two- or 3-inch heels which aren't too pointed provide the most elegant walk, and are much less harmful to the spinal column, which undergoes enough stress without the added burden of stiletto heels!

As soon as your shoes start to wear out, get them repaired. Heels and soles in good condition are essential for keeping your back healthy and your walk fluid and elegant.

3 YOUR MOVEMENTS

If you want to acquire a magnetic personality, your movements must be elegant and balanced.

Let's say you move a lot — you make sweeping, exaggerated gestures. You have to learn to control them and limit them to some extent. Overwhelming and uncontrolled gestures generally indicate an extroverted, flamboyant character, which can become somewhat tiring to the people around you. If you fall into this category, learn to moderate your movements!

On the other hand, if you're an introvert, you're probably very stingy with your gestures. In this case, you have to learn to liberate your body to some extent. It's as though you're wearing an emotional and physical straitjacket, which you must absolutely tear to shreds if you want to liberate the magnetism and personal charm that, at the moment, lies sleeping somewhere deep inside you.

Controlling your gestures automatically means controlling your emotions, because our movements are a reflection of the way we feel.

Become aware of your movements

Would you know how to describe your gestures? Are you aware of them? In order to tone them down or amplify them, you must become familiar with them. If you have doubts, the following test will help you to classify methodically the way you move in various situations.

TEST: BECOME AWARE OF YOUR GESTURES

Here is a list of descriptions that could apply to your gestures:

Generous	Uncertain
Brusque	Slow
Restrained	Clumsy
Erratic	Methodical

Exaggerated   Precise
Insufficient   Jerky
Rapid   Dry

Answer the following questions with three of those descriptions.

1   When you wash in the morning, your gestures are:
    1
    2
    3
2   When you pack your luggage your movements are:
3   When you're getting ready to go out and realize you're running late, your movements are:
4   When you're gluing a broken object together, your movements are:
5   When you're relaxing with friends, your gestures are:
6   When you're working and you know someone is watching you, your movements are:
7   If you're sitting at the head of a large table at a dinner party, your movements are:

Now take the qualities that appear three or more times on your list and write them down on a sheet of paper. You now have a profile of the way you move your body. You are ready for an exercise that will teach you to be totally conscious of your gestures.

EXERCISE: MIME

This exercise is somewhat special because you can adapt it to any anxiety-causing situation, whenever you instinctively feel the need for more self-assurance.

1   Get comfortable in front of your mirror.

2 Imagine that you've been invited to a party. You are standing, holding a glass in your hand, in the midst of a conversation with another guest. A waiter approaches with a tray of hors d'oeuvres.

3 Now analyze every one of your gestures:
- You smile at the person holding the tray and look them straight in the eye.
- Without moving your hands, you glance down at the contents of the tray.
- You slowly lift your free hand to the tray and reach for the hors d'oeuvre nearest you.
- You calmly lift the hors d'oeuvre and smile at the person you were talking to before taking a bite.

This very simple, but very effective exercise can be adapted to any situation. You could imagine, for example, that you're at the checkout in a supermarket, paying for your groceries and arranging them in boxes.

Make a list of all the situations where you are consistently clumsy, and adapt them to this exercise. Then look for results after just a few days of practice.

EXERCISE: STAYING CALM

You may belong to the category of people who gesticulate a lot when they talk. This exercise will help you stay calm when you speak to friends or colleagues.

1 Get out your faithful old mirror and sit down comfortably in front of it.

2 Talk to yourself about your day, or about any other subject that comes to mind, without making the slightest gesture. If you move your little finger, start again.

The first session shouldn't last more than 3 minutes. When you get used to it, you can extend the duration a little. If, after a few weeks, you're able to tell yourself a story lasting 15 minutes without moving at all, then you're cured. You will face your friends and colleagues calmly, and be composed and convincing.

In this way you learn to economize your movements in a natural way.

A further piece of advice for making your gestures more confident and flowing: read a book on social etiquette. We mentioned this in the previous chapter on shyness. There, we suggested it as a way to gain more self-assurance when communicating with other people. But how many clumsy gestures do you think are caused by a lack of self-assurance? Knowing exactly what and what not to do in a given situation will help you master your gestures, making them more supple and more studied. This will add to your sense of security, and you'll be more self-assured.

How's your handshake?

You're probably aware that shaking hands is a very important gesture. It is one of the ways people form an immediate judgement of someone.

Could you describe your handshake? (If you can't, ask someone else to do it for you.) Write it down. My handshake is . . .

Have you ever shaken someone's hand, only to have your fingers crushed in a vice-like grasp? Has a handshake ever reminded you of a dead fish — limp, clammy and cold?

The ideal handshake is firm and dry. Observe your own, and make an effort to correct it if necessary. Keep in mind that a handshake is one of the pieces of the puzzle that defines our personality.

4 YOUR FACE

Your face is usually what others see first of you. You may be wearing the most impeccable clothes, walk like Greta Garbo, study your every gesture — if your facial expression remains closed, if it's vacant or if your mouth is pursed with tension, you will have no success attracting others.

So let's spend a little time discussing the 'mask' we present to the exterior world every day. (Did you know that the word 'personality' comes from 'persona', which means mask?)

Get rid of your mannerisms

We almost all have certain mannerisms. Some people blink too often, others frown or wrinkle their nose for no reason, some people are constantly biting their lips, and so on.,

Mannerisms are the physical manifestations of psychological problems, often with deep underlying causes. What can you do to get rid of them?

Find the cause

Ideally you would, with the help of a therapist, look for the cause of your mannerism.

'I'm not going to consult a psychotherapist just because of a nervous tic!' you say.

Why not? If a mannerism is ruining your life by making you look ridiculous, if people make snide or condescending remarks — do something about it!

If, on the other hand, you consider your mannerisms too mild to make you the butt of other people's ridicule, or if you already know what their causes are (left-handed people, for example, often have a twitch in their eye), then here are a few instructions you can follow to control them, or even get rid of them completely:

- Pull your hair down so that it covers as much of your face as possible. Imagine that the hairs touching your forehead and cheeks are live 'twitch detonators'.

- Get your eyesight checked regularly by an ophthalmologist. It's very important.
- Wear sunglasses (good quality, of course) when the sun is strong — and ONLY for the sun.
- Massage your face every day, using the ends of your fingers and moving gently upwards. Use non-greasy cream to massage (men too!). Creams with a Vitamin E base are excellent for the skin, and aren't greasy at all.
- Smile often, laugh out loud, let yourself feel joyous. There's nothing better than relaxing for getting rid of nervous mannerisms.

Be aware of the way you look at others

What kind of gaze do you have? Steady or shifting, warm or ice-cold, straight, amused, sad . . .? Have you ever counted the number of adjectives there are to describe a person's gaze? Thousands!

You must have noticed that in most novels, whatever their literary merit, if there's ever a single trait mentioned about a character, it's their eyes. Many authors omit detailed descriptions of their characters, but always, without exception, furnish the reader with some indication of the character's gaze, eye colour and shape.

Eyes are the primary intermediary between our brains and the external world. They are given special consideration in mythology — you may have heard of the 'third eye' of the orientals, or the Cyclops with their single eyes in Greek mythology.

All this is to let you know that you must not neglect the way you look at people. Eye contact is one of the main ways your personality is expressed.

How should you look at others?

Popular opinion decrees that a shifting gaze is the reflection of a shy, or even dishonest personality, while a frank, steady gaze automatically denotes strength and goodness. In reality, it's more subtle than that.

Improve Your Physical Appearance

Shy people often have an aggressive, almost insolent way of looking at others. They feel constantly on the defensive, persuaded as they are that others consider them to be inferior. So they try to compensate and assert themselves by adding an element of disdain to their gaze. This is a mistake! Aggressiveness, disdain, insolence or arrogance can betray a lack of security just as easily as a lowered or shifting gaze.

If you always force yourself to look people in the eyes, you may find yourself staring and making other people uncomfortable. They in turn react by escaping, or by becoming aggressive.

You may know that many mammals, notably cats, use eye contact as a preliminary to attack, which follows in due course — the first cat to lower its eyes signals its submission to the other. It has been reported that looking certain species of monkeys in the eye provokes them to rage.

Here's an exercise to help you direct and judiciously control the fire in your eyes.

EXERCISE: HOW TO DEVELOP AN 'IRRESISTIBLE GAZE'

---

1. Get comfortable in front of your mirror and look at yourself.

2. Run your gaze over your entire face, observing the corners of your eyes, your forehead, the base of your nose, your chin and cheeks.

3. Come back to your eyes. Look yourself in the eyes, concentrating your vision on the area around your eyes. Persevere for a few minutes. Do the exercise regularly, once or twice a day if possible.

Some people complain that they find it tiring to stare at another person for any length of time. Our eyes are subjected to a lot of stress. They are damaged by the gases and toxic pollutants in our environment, by the negative effects of certain kinds of lighting, by the sun's rays, by certain common activities (reading, working with a computer screen or a microscope, doing fine sewing or embroidery, driving at night, etc.).

Doing eye exercises is an effective way to combat what is called 'ocular fatigue'. Here's one that's very easy — you can do it practically anywhere.

EXERCISE: STRENGTHENING THE EYE MUSCLES

1. Sit or stand in front of a medium-sized frame — it could contain a painting, a window, a screen, a mirror, etc.

2. Keep your head completely immobile, and move your eyes to each of the four corners of the frame, going around 12 times. You'll soon be able to stare at an object or person for a long time without feeling an irresistible desire to look elsewhere.

3. If your problem is blinking too much, do the same exercise using a shiny surface.

5 YOUR VOICE

Your voice is just as powerful a weapon as your gaze. It can charm and soothe, or irritate and repel. Ideally, your voice should be calm, without putting other people to sleep!

Many of us are afflicted with voices that society inexplicably deems unpleasant. I am referring especially to shrill, high-pitched voices. If you're one of those people, you probably regret having a shrill voice, and do your best to lower it. *Stop!* Unless you use your voice at its proper pitch, you'll damage your vocal chords. Accept the voice you were born with. It's

Improve Your Physical Appearance

yours, it matches your personality, just as the colour of your eyes automatically matches your skin colour.

Despite the hasty judgements that are simply the result of a snobbish attitude in society, some high-pitched voices are rich and well modulated, and possess none of the shrill, piercing, strident tones usually associated with them. They can be very pleasant to the ear. On the other hand, a deep voice can be rasping or snarling, inciting a desire in whoever is listening to help the speaker before he or she succumbs to a fit of coughing.

So whether your voice is high or low, don't be too hasty in judging its merits or faults!

A pleasant and soothing voice is certainly an advantage in life. If you drew up a list of the people you know whom you admire, you'd probably notice that one of the qualities that draws you to them is their voice.

Practise on your voice

Anyone who aspires to a career in theatre must study diction, but courses in diction are not just for actors. If you think your voice needs work, sign up for an elementary course in diction. In a short time, you'll see people turn their heads to listen whenever you start talking in a group. The improvement will be nothing short of miraculous!

Other people don't hear your voice the same way you do. Therefore, to know exactly what kind of voice you have, you have to tape yourself (using a good quality machine). If you've never listened to yourself on tape before, get ready for a surprise. You'll be hearing your voice as others hear it.

The voice adds shades of meaning to a verbal message. It can even transform a message completely. The story goes that Lord (Laurence) Olivier was able to make his friends cry by reciting the alphabet!

If you haven't got the inclination, or the means, to pay for a course in diction, here's a short exercise that will help you improve the quality of your voice.

How to Develop Charisma & Personal Magnetism

EXERCISE: HOW TO TRAIN YOUR VOICE

1. Using a tape machine to record your voice, read a text of about 300 words in your mother tongue. (You may also want to work on texts in other languages.)

2. Listen to yourself. Take notes, deciding what you don't like about your voice.

3. Read through the text again, keeping your notes in mind. Correct yourself. Take your time. Try to slow your pace down, and enunciate carefully, while sounding natural.

4. After a few days, stop reading the text. Sit down with your microphone every day after work, for example, and talk about your day. Try to stick to the point, without being too dry. Listen to yourself talking, articulate carefully, be natural.

If you do the exercise regularly for a few months, you should notice a significant improvement in your diction and voice quality.

You can send cassettes to your friends instead of writing to them. Tape stories for your children. Learn to dictate your mail. Rest assured that an articulate, calm, collected and friendly voice will be of enormous use to you throughout your life. People will like you, they'll listen to you and trust you much more easily if you know how to use your voice to charm them.

SUMMARY

You did the test on physical well-being, and found that something wasn't quite right in your relationship to your body.

One of the essential elements of personal charm is a sense of physical well-being. If you're uncomfortable with your body, you'll never be able to influence others in a positive way through the magnetism of your personality.

Improve Your Physical Appearance

Work to improve the elements that make up your 'allure': your posture, your gestures, your gaze and your voice.

All these elements can be easily corrected by special exercises. You'll start noticing a difference in just a few weeks. Without knowing exactly why or how, you will have acquired the charm and allure you were lacking. You'll have the impression your clothes look better, others will find you more attractive, more open, and you'll be well on the way to achieving a harmonious relationship with your body.

CHAPTER SIX

The Keys to an Irresistible Appearance

Now that you've learned how to control your attitudes and mannerisms, ask yourself whether your appearance is creating a favourable impression or not. You've worked to acquire the bearing of a monarch, a charming voice and a bewitching gaze. Perfect! But now's not the time to sit back and stop. There are two more elements which also play a fundamental role in forming not only the image you have of yourself, but the one you present to other people as well.

These two elements are your body itself, and its material envelope — in other words, the clothes you wear.

'Why,' you ask, 'should I be concerned with those aspects if it's true that physical beauty doesn't have much to do with charisma?'

Good question! Let's look at this line of reasoning. Charismatic persons are not necessarily gifted with the physique of Greek gods. They radiate an inner charm which is not dependent on a pleasing exterior to be effective. On that we agree. However, magnetic charm is subject to a need for 'corporeal comfort'. To charm others, you first have to feel good about yourself.

We repeat that when a person feels good about him or herself, it's because he has accepted his physique, whatever shape it may be. If you haven't accepted yours, there must be something about your appearance that you don't like, which prevents you from liking — and accepting — yourself.

What is it?

That's what you'll find out in the next few minutes.

The Keys to an Irresistible Appearance

1 WHAT'S WRONG WITH YOUR BODY?

Step one: identify your physical defects

Find a room where you won't be disturbed, get undressed and stand in front of your full-length mirror. Inspect your body. What's wrong with it? Be merciless. Make a list of the things you don't like about your body.

Don't be surprised if the list isn't very long. This is probably because in the past you tended to exaggerate the importance of one or two physical defects, to the point of believing that you hated your body.

Now that you know exactly what you find displeasing about your body, look for the solutions to your problems. For example, plastic surgery can rectify most imperfections, from a bumpy nose to overly large breasts.

If you have a recurring skin problem, don't consult a dermatologist (who will likely treat only the symptoms and not the cause), but rather a general practitioner, who will perform a battery of tests and then recommend you to an endocrinologist, or a neurologist, or a dietitian, as your case requires.

Uneven or stained teeth can be corrected by a specialist. An optician can help you choose glasses that suit you better. A beautician can determine what type of hairstyle complements your face best. For each problem there's a solution.

Next to each problem or imperfection, write down the solution that, in theory, seems best.

Step two: the moment of truth

There are two possibilities open to you:

- accept the imperfection
- apply the solution

'That doesn't leave much of a choice!' you say.

But it does.

Think hard about what you've written down. Analyse each problem and each solution calmly. Here's an example of the kind of reasoning you should adopt:

'Am I ready to undergo plastic surgery, which can be costly and painful, to change my nose (or get rid of the bags under my eyes, or enlarge my breasts, etc.)?'

'Am I prepared to wear braces for months or even years in order to adjust the position of two or three teeth?'

'Am I prepared to wear tinted contact lenses all day long because I don't like the colour of my eyes?'

'Am I prepared to spend half a day at the hairdresser's every week or two weeks, in order to maintain my new hair colour and style?'

If you decide that your minor defects are not important enough to warrant the intervention of a specialist, then make up your mind once and for all. From now on you have no reason to complain about an imperfection because you've voluntarily, and in full awareness, chosen to accept it. Tell yourself:

'I accept this imperfection.'

On the other hand, if you feel ready to undergo the inconveniences — financial and other — associated with the solution, then don't put it off. Don't look for any false pretexts, like 'I haven't got the time right now . . .' or 'I haven't got the money.' Time and money don't count for much when the success of your whole life is at stake!

A physical defect is no longer a defect as soon as you are able to accept it. And you can rest assured that if you accept it, other people will accept it too.

Your smile, your benevolent attitude, the friendliness in your eyes, the suppleness and elegance of your movements — qualities such as these are more than enough to make people forget about the size of your nose, or a few premature wrinkles, or the way your ears stick out a little, or the faded colour of your eyes or your dull hair.

2 THE SOLUTION TO MOST PROBLEMS

Exercise.

'Oh God, not again!' you say. You can hardly open a book these days without hearing about the benefits of exercise.

If you've been exercising regularly for years, you don't need to read the following paragraphs, unless you need to reconfirm your belief that exercise can cure most disorders. And it's almost certain that your lack of self-confidence has nothing to do with the way you see your body. The cause of your shyness does not stem from your body image.

On the other hand, if you're one of the many people who don't like their body, then it's time to get off your butt and do something about it.

Many excellent books are available which describe the mental and physical benefits of regular exercise. So one of the best things you can do for yourself is to buy one of these books, and start practising the programme of exercise it recommends.

Meanwhile, here is a list (far from complete) of what exercise can do for you:

- it improves muscle tone
- it enhances cardiovascular capacity
- it reduces cholesterol levels in the blood
- it combats hypertension
- it keeps you slim and fights obesity
- it increases your 'energy reserve'
- it is an anti-depressant
- it improves the quality of your sleep
- it reduces appetite
- it results in a feeling of physical well-being
- it improves your skin

- it reinforces the immune system and helps fight disease
- it slows down the aging process and prolongs life

Don't you agree it would be a good idea for you to start exercising?

To acquire the 'magnetic personality' you dream of having, you must create an impression of well-being, and consider your body as a friend. Train it, make it strong. It will soon become firm and supple. You'll drop those unsightly rolls of fat, or if you're too thin, you'll develop the muscle tissue you need to look and feel your best.

In addition, you'll overflow with energy and enthusiasm. You'll soon notice that you need less time to do the same tasks. And you won't be bothered by those nagging colds that can make the winter months so miserable.

By fighting obesity, illness and fatigue, exercise will give you a renewed sense of confidence in your body. You'll feel 10 times better than before! Fresh blood will flow through your veins, like new sap in spring.

You'll find all the advice you need in one of the many excellent books written for people who have decided to get back into shape and do at least a minimum of exercise after years of inactivity.

You should be aware, however, that every year of inactivity requires a month's training if you want to get back into reasonable shape. Which means that if you haven't done anything for 12 years, you'll need a year of training to get you back into some semblance of proper condition.

How to go about starting a training programme

Here is some practical advice, which is so simple many authors forget to mention it in their books on exercise:

- Set realistic goals. Don't be too hard on yourself. You are your best friend. Don't aggravate yourself.
- Find an activity you like doing now. Don't, for example, take up tennis because your parents insisted you play tennis

when you were 12 years old.
- Choose an activity (or a few activities, if that's what you want) that you have a real affinity for. What do we mean by this? Well, for example, if you're a solid, well-built person, you'd probably feel better doing endurance sports (like cycling, swimming, aerobics, cross-country skiing, etc.) rather than sports which require speed and agility (gymnastics, tennis, martial arts, etc.). On the other hand, if you have a wiry build, you'll certainly realise after a few training sessions that you move quickly and with precision. Take advantage of your natural gifts.
- Also look for an activity that is compatible with your frame of mind. If you don't like competition, choose activities you can do alone, quietly, or with other people who are just as uninterested in competing as you are. And vice versa. If you don't take your personality into account, you risk getting discouraged quickly. Don't forget that sport is not a synonym for competition.
- It's often said that it's easier to train in a group. This is true for some people, but not for everyone. Many people work a lot better when they're alone. They don't feel inhibited, and can let go more easily, giving the most of themselves. If you're one of those people, don't think twice about developing your own training programme and working alone.
- Avoid training with people who are way above or way below your performance level. In the former case, you'll get discouraged, in the later you won't progress as quickly as you'd like. Train with people who are at the same level as you are, or alone.
- Whatever sport you do, learn to breathe properly. Any exercise will seem a lot easier if you know how to breathe correctly. A little later on there's a very simple breathing exercise that you can use for whatever sport you choose.
- Don't scrimp on equipment. Even if you find sports equipment and clothes cost a lot, tell yourself that you're making a good long-term investment. You'll quickly

appreciate both the physical and psychological benefits of having good equipment.

A few exercise ideas to improve muscle tone
In the interim between now and the start of your official training programme, here are some suggestions for exercises that you can do any time during the day, at home, or at work.

EXERCISE: FIRM UP YOUR THIGHS

1   At any hour of the day, sitting in a chair with your back straight and your legs folded at right angles to your body, breathe in deeply and count to 10.

2   Now squeeze your thighs tightly together and hold them that way, while simultaneously breathing out slowly and counting to 10.

3   Release your thigh muscles. Do the exercise at least 20 times.

EXERCISE: IMPROVE YOUR HANDSHAKE

Many of us complain that we don't have strong enough hands. We always have trouble opening tightly closed jars, tearing cardboard or plastic wrapping, and so on. This exercise will make those everyday little efforts a lot easier. It'll also make your hands look better, and strengthen your handshake.

1   Collect a pile of scrap paper.
2   Crumple the whole pile into little balls, one sheet at a time. Take a sheet in each hand, and crumple them until you're left with the smallest, most tightly packed ball possible. Do this exercise at least three times a week.

The Keys to an Irresistible Appearance

You'll be amazed to see how much stronger the muscles in your hands get, slowly but surely. Not only will exercising become easier, you'll also find that the shape of your hands and forearms will improve.

It's important to develop muscle tone in the upper part of the body. Because we're bipeds, we're forced to use our legs, even if only minimally. But we often neglect our shoulders and arms, which produces an imbalance in our bodies.

If you make an effort to eliminate this imbalance, you'll move more gracefully, your shoulders will be straight and your chest firm (which is just as important for women as for men). You'll create an impression of harmony and balance, you'll feel more sturdy on your feet, and more comfortable with your body. Isn't this one of the goals you wish to attain?

Breathing

Breathing is an essential component of physical hygiene. Unfortunately, the only reason three quarters of the population breathe is to prevent themselves from suffocating. They are unaware that, with each inhalation and exhalation of breath, they can clean their system, nourish their muscles and improve their cardiovascular capacity.

If you undertake an exercise programme, you absolutely must learn how to breathe. If you don't, you won't accomplish very much. Breathing correctly not only makes training easier, it also speeds up your progress by combating fatigue.

How to breathe

The first rule is that you have to breathe with your stomach. Abdominal breathing is the only kind of breathing that is effective. So practise breathing regularly by lifting your stomach and filling it with air. Then empty your lungs completely by breathing out slowly and flattening your stomach.

EXERCISE: BREATHING

This exercise will give you a great feeling of well-being, and at the same time improve your endurance. Yet it's childishly simple:

1. Breathe in deeply, counting to eight.
2. Hold your breath and count to five.
3. Breathe out deeply and count to eight.

That's it!

Do the exercise at least a dozen times a day, anywhere you happen to have a moment.

All exercising becomes a lot easier when you know how to breathe. You don't lose your breath as quickly, you don't tire your heart out needlessly, and you avoid those very unpleasant stitches in your side.

3 LEARN TO DRESS

You would agree that clothes, for what they're worth, are an indication of your personality. They are, in a way, part of yourself.

You have probably noticed on a number of occasions that the way a person was dressed did a lot to influence what others thought of that person.

What about you? How do you relate to clothes?

TEST: YOUR PROFILE AS A DRESSER

Answer the following questions honestly, with a simple yes or no in each case.

The Keys to an Irresistible Appearance

1. Do you have problems choosing your clothes when you go shopping?
2. Do you hesitate for a long time before buying an article of clothing?
3. Are there any clothes in your wardrobe that you regret having bought, and that you never wear?
4. Do you think that if you had more money, you'd be better dressed?
5. When buying your clothes, do you follow your instinct, or do you let others influence you (sales people, relatives, friends, etc.)?

Results
Give yourself 1 point for each affirmative answer.

If you scored between 3 and 5 points:
You have a lot to learn about dressing. You don't really know what suits you and what doesn't, and you don't value your clothes very much. You hesitate too much, and your judgment is faulty. You probably let other people influence you, because of laziness, or because of your defeatist attitude. You've got to take charge. You'll start enjoying clothes when you've learned how to dress yourself.

If you scored 1 or 2 points:
You're on the right track. However, you probably still hesitate and make some mistakes when you buy clothes. You underestimate your potential in this area.

If you answered 'No' to all questions:
You know all you need to know about dressing. You're a careful shopper, you think about what to buy but you don't hesitate too much. You probably commit very few errors. Congratulations!

As you see, your answers to the above questions enable you to determine your strong and weak points as far as dressing is concerned. Now you know if you're an impulsive or a thoughtful buyer, if you're decided or hesitant, careful or likely to make mistakes.

It seems that the vast majority of people who wish to develop their charisma dress so that they are noticed. Look at the people around you — that man who always wears bow ties, or the woman whose earrings are as big as hubcaps, or that young man with holes carefully cut in the knees of his jeans — these are people you see every day.

Yet these people are making a mistake! All they're doing is attracting attention. A charismatic person does not simply want to attract attention!

To maximize your personal charm, you should dress in a discreet but becoming way, either in the current fashion or along classical lines, depending on your taste and figure.

Above all, you should project the image of being comfortable in the clothes you're wearing. Because clothes are like your second skin. And to the people you come into contact with, your clothes are an important part of your personality.

Minor errors to be avoided

Now let's take a look at some of the questions in the test individually. Each one deals with a fundamental problem in the area of dressing.

Question 4, for example: do you think you'd dress better if you had more money? Did you say yes?

Well, you were wrong!

Think about the people you know for a moment. Some make cheap clothes look like designer originals. Others, who have the money to buy the originals, still look like they're wearing sacks.

This doesn't mean that it's always better to shop for bargains. If you can afford to buy good material and well-cut clothing, go right ahead! But one thing you should know — if you're not comfortable in your clothes, no matter what they cost, you'll never radiate that aura of confidence and well-being that is an essential element of charisma.

Another important question: do you let other people influence you when you buy clothes?

If you do, you're making a mistake.

You're the only one who can decide whether an article of clothing suits you or not. The impression should be immediate, undeniable and decisive — as soon as you try it on, you 'know'.

Don't ask someone else: 'Do you think it suits me?' Don't let the sales people influence you — they usually don't care whether you look like a king or a clown!

How to choose

An article of clothing is composed of three elements: colour, cut and material.

Rule 1: Determine the colours that suit you

This wasn't such an easy thing to do, until a few years ago. We had no guidelines; we'd buy things because we liked the colour, but we didn't know that the colour didn't suit us. Or, if we thought we knew our colour, we'd stick to it, until everything in our wardrobe was monotone!

Today, as you probably know, a system has been developed whereby you can determine exactly which colours and shades work for you and which don't. The test consists of placing a number of different coloured scarves next to the face (without any makeup) and deciding which are most becoming. A number of different companies operate this service — look in the phone book or ask around.

Rule 2: Choose your materials once and for all

A material's texture is an important element. We all have affinities for certain materials. Some people prefer synthetic fibres, others natural fibres. Don't forget that natural materials usually require more care (ironing, washing by hand, etc.).

Rule 3: Choose the styles that suit you best
This is a delicate question. Few people have a figure that is suited to all types of styles. We have to make a choice.

The secret of elegance is to choose a cut that complements your figure. If you are doubtful, i.e. if you don't know what suits you and what doesn't, consult a specialist in fashion design or production. Some of the companies that do colour analysis also provide guidelines on style. An expert can explain why certain styles are better for you, and why you should avoid others. Don't be shy about asking for help — like almost anything else, knowing how to dress is something you can learn to do.

You'll be able to minimize the impact of your body's imperfections, and enhance its qualities. Consult your mirror often — it won't lie.

The 'big clean-up'
If your answer to question 3 was yes, then your wardrobe is probably overflowing with clothes that you never wear for a variety of reasons.

Take them all out and examine them. Ask yourself why you don't wear them. Make it a lesson for the future — let these clothes become a symbol of the mistakes you won't make anymore.

SUMMARY

You now know what you need to do to dress properly and feel good about yourself, so that you can be as charming as you'd like to be.

You listed your physical faults, and the solutions available to you. After studying the options calmly, you made your decision: either do what is necessary to resolve the problem, or accept yourself as you are, once and for all!

If you want your body to exude harmony and health, it's essential that you exercise. Read a couple of books on the subject, written for beginners, and develop your own training programme. Your entire being will benefit.

Finally, take care of your body's outer covering, i.e. your clothes. If you belong to the category of people who don't really know how to dress, or who think that nothing suits them, know that a solution does exist. Learn which colours and styles are right for you, and remind yourself that your clothes are, for the people you meet, a reflection of your personality.

Don't let them down!

CHAPTER SEVEN

How to Master Your Emotions

Why is it important that you learn to master your emotions?

Think about the attitudes of people you know, whom you judge to be charismatic. Have you ever seen them sputtering with indignation, or ranting angrily, or sweating or blushing from head to foot, or running around like a headless chicken?

No, on the contrary. One of the aspects of their personality that attracts you the most is the impression they give of staying calm and serene no matter what befalls them. A feeling of profound harmony and balance emanates from their being. Although they are sensitive, they possess the faculty, either innate or acquired, of being able to control their emotions.

We're not talking about eliminating emotion from your life. Emotion leads to action, and makes us sensitive to others' needs. It is an essential human trait, which only becomes harmful if we allow it to snowball and overwhelm us, instead of trying to master it.

WHAT ARE THE CONCRETE ADVANTAGES OF MASTERING YOUR EMOTIONS?

1 You won't suffer from stage fright

If you're a shy person, if you lack confidence, then you've certainly experienced that most horrible of uncontrolled emotions — stage fright — at one time or another in your life. You may have failed an oral exam because of it, or lost a job you wanted a lot.

Perhaps you've never dared to express your feelings for someone who is very dear to you.

By learning to get rid of stage fright, you'll look at life in a completely new way. Don't be ashamed! Even people as famous as Marlene Dietrich and Steven Spielberg admit that, at certain moments in their career, they had to overcome terrific feelings of stage fright.

2 You'll multiply your energy

Uncontrolled emotions use up a terrific amount of physical and mental energy.

Physical reactions caused by emotions can be exhausting: rashes, trembling of the hands and legs, gasping for breath, excessive perspiration, tachycardia, nausea, insomnia and other signs of emotion consume an enormous amount of energy. If you don't learn to control your emotions, you'll find yourself completely and needlessly exhausted at the end of the day.

The charismatic people you know always look fresh and ready for anything. Haven't you often racked your brain, trying to figure out how they do it? Well, it's due in large part to their mastering of emotions, which allows them to recuperate energy more easily, and to be stronger and more discerning when faced with the unpleasant surprises life throws our way from time to time.

3 You'll be healthier

This aspect is a natural result of the preceding one. Obviously, if you waste less energy on exaggerated emotional reactions, you'll have more energy to fight disease and depression.

Stress will have less of an effect on you, and you'll be less susceptible to its unpleasant symptoms, such as hypertension, skin problems, allergies, migraines, etc. You'll exude health and well-being, and will become the envy of those around you.

4 You'll gain credibility

If shouting, crying and gnashing your teeth are part of your everyday behaviour, don't be surprised if people stop taking you seriously.

You're always 'crying wolf' and 'your bark is a lot stronger than your bite!'

Smash this image of yourself into a thousand pieces. Re-establish your credibility!

Only calm and collected people, who create an impression of balance and wisdom, are capable of convincing others, and of being respected and admired. Be honest with yourself. Aren't you more likely to listen to someone who communicates what s/he has to say in a firm and calm manner, rather than someone who gets overly excited, goes all red and stammers out a string of jumbled phrases?

WHAT IS YOUR EMOTIONAL PROFILE?

You'll find the answer to this question by doing the following test.

TEST: EMOTIVITY

Answer these questions:

1. Do you prefer working:
   a) *alone*
   b) *in a group*
   c) *as part of a small team*

2. When you watch a sad film, do you cry:
   a) *often*
   b) *never*
   c) *sometimes*

3. If you find yourself in an untenable or absurd situation, confronted by an unreasonable colleague, do you:
   a) *leave the scene as quickly as possible*
   b) *become aggressive*
   c) *ask the company director to intercede*

4. Do you bring your professional problems home with you, or your domestic problems to work:
   a) *often*
   b) *rarely*
   c) *sometimes*

5. How do you react to failure:
   a) *you analyze the causes of your failure*
   b) *you try to stop thinking about it as quickly as possible*
   c) *you become very depressed*

6. You serve a meat dish to some guests which seems to be slightly off:
   a) *you're so embarrassed, your whole night is ruined*
   b) *you make a joke out of it, and order a pizza*
   c) *you hope that no one will notice*

7. Do you keep sentimental souvenirs (love letters, school mementos, travel souvenirs, etc.):
   a) *you hold on to everything*
   b) *you keep only a very few souvenirs*
   c) *you keep absolutely nothing*

8. You find out that someone has been criticising you:
   a) *you tell yourself that the person has every right to do so*
   b) *you pretend you know nothing about it*
   c) *you call the person immediately and demand an explanation*

9. Do you suffer from anxiety:
   a) *never*
   b) *sometimes*
   c) *often*

10. Are you afraid of the future:
    a) *not at all*
    b) *a little*
    c) *very much*

11. If your boss reprimands you for a mistake you made:
    a) *you get upset*
    b) *you try to place the blame on someone else*
    c) *you explain why you acted as you did, under the circumstances*

12. The mechanic you paid to fix your car didn't do the work properly:
    a) *you get angry and threaten never to talk to him again*
    b) *you firmly demand that he redo the work*
    c) *you change mechanics*

13. Do you think that other people:
    a) *underestimate you*
    b) *appreciate your true worth*
    c) *overestimate you*

14. When you have some exacting work to do:
    a) *you get distracted easily*
    b) *you concentrate to the point where you're almost oblivious to everything around you*
    c) *you concentrate, while remaining receptive to your surroundings*

15. Your spouse blames you for:
    a) *not expressing your emotions enough*
    b) *being too emotional*
    c) *being too logical*

16. When faced with an emergency:
    a) *you deal with the problem step by step*
    b) *you panic*
    c) *you react automatically, without thinking*

17. Your anger is:
    a) *explosive*
    b) *cold*
    c) *rare*

18. When you meet a friend you haven't seen for a long time:
    a) *you greet him/her with great enthusiasm*

How to Master Your Emotions

    b) *you express your pleasure in seeing them again, while remaining reserved*
    c) *you greet him/her as if you'd just seen them the night before*

19 When you have to discipline someone:
    a) *you listen to the person's arguments, without letting yourself be swayed*
    b) *you refuse to listen to any explanations*
    c) *you let yourself be persuaded and forget about the reprimand*

20 When you have to speak in public:
    a) *you suffer from terrible stage fright*
    b) *you calmly express what you have to say*
    c) *your nervousness disappears as soon as you start speaking*

Results

QUESTION	POINTS SCORED		
1	a = 5	b = 3	c = 1
2	a = 5	b = 1	c = 3
3	a = 1	b = 5	c = 3
4	a = 5	b = 1	c = 3
5	a = 3	b = 1	c = 5
6	a = 5	b = 3	c = 1
7	a = 5	b = 3	c = 1
8	a = 3	b = 1	c = 5
9	a = 1	b = 3	c = 5
10	a = 1	b = 3	c = 5
11	a = 1	b = 5	c = 3
12	a = 5	b = 3	c = 1
13	a = 5	b = 3	c = 1
14	a = 5	b = 1	c = 3
15	a = 1	b = 5	c = 3
16	a = 3	b = 5	c = 1
17	a = 5	b = 1	c = 3
18	a = 5	b = 3	c = 1
19	a = 3	b = 1	c = 5
20	a = 5	b = 1	c = 3

If you scored between 70 and 100 points:
You are too emotional.

You don't really know how to control your emotions, and it's possible you're paying the price in your relations with others. You shout and smoulder, but when the time for action comes, you do an about-face and react with confusion. People around you never know what to expect from you. Your reactions are often exaggerated, out of proportion to the situation at hand. You react by becoming either too aggressive or depressed.

You fluctuate rapidly between states of euphoria and despair. People close to you may find you somewhat tiring. And, in fact, you are tiring yourself out.

You are probably under the impression — and rightly so — that people don't appreciate you fully. Your mercurial character probably offends quite a lot of people, who under other conditions could benefit from your company.

Learn to master your emotions. Your life will be calmer, more serene, more balanced. You'll have more harmonious relationships. You'll gain the credibility of those around you.

If you scored between 40 and 69 points:
You are emotionally balanced.

You may throw a little tantrum from time to time, you may occasionally be troubled or unable to concentrate. But you know how to express your feelings without embarrassing other people. You hold no grudges against yourself or against others. You are at peace. You demonstrate an acute sense of objectivity.

Even though you occasionally suffer from twinges of stage fright, you've learned how to master it. Your personal life is probably serene, and your relations with people in general are relaxed. People respect you, and very probably admire you.

People feel relaxed in your company because they know what to expect of you, without considering you boring or predictable.

If you scored less than 40 points:
You are suppressing your emotions.

You are completely governed by reason and duty. You are conscientious and determined to see everything you undertake through to the end. You are an excellent strategist. Your logic is tried and tested.

You've probably never become enraged. However, you are capable of a cold and dangerous kind of anger. You often manifest your aggressiveness by cutting yourself off from others, nurturing your animosity. You are capable of enduring hatred. You forget neither your errors, nor those of others.

People find you cold, and lacking in compassion. Even those you're very close to and love sincerely don't know what you're really thinking — you are so undemonstrative, they wonder how you feel about them.

Controlling your emotions by no means requires suppressing them completely. You just have to prevent them from becoming too important, from taking up too much space in your life.

Exaggerated suppression of emotion results in exactly the same kind of symptoms as being overly demonstrative. You exhaust yourself by constantly keeping everything inside, you become a perfect victim for high blood pressure, migraines, cardiac and digestive problems, insomnia, allergies, skin problems, and so on.

You are in a perpetual state of tension. Since you don't know how to express it, you develop various physical symptoms in order to manifest it. You're like an elastic band, stretched to breaking-point. The day it snaps, your friends better steer clear!

But there's hope for you yet. Keep on reading, and make use of the advice you find in this chapter. It applies as much to you as to people who can't control their emotions at all.

FOUR GOLDEN RULES FOR ATTAINING EMOTIONAL BALANCE

1 Learn to relax
You can easily understand how fatigue, mental or physical

tension, nervousness or anxiety is a needless waste of your energy. You knew that already. Learn to relax your body as well as your mind, and get rid of all those poisons that have been steadily draining your energy reserves.

All relaxation exercises which teach you to empty your mind and relax your muscles are beneficial. You can do them in the evening when you come home from work (just make sure that you're not disturbed for at least half an hour) or at night before going to bed.

You could also take a course in yoga or some form of meditation. Not only will you learn to relax, you'll improve your motor co-ordination and your psychological equilibrium.

Meanwhile, here are a few ideas for relaxation exercises.

EXERCISE: MUSCLE RELAXATION

1   Stretch out on your bed, or on a carpet, with a small pillow under your head. Adjust the room temperature so you're not cold, and close your eyes.

2   To relax all your muscles completely, you have to start by tensing them up. This is very important.

3   Start with your face. Contract your facial muscles. Maintain the tension while you count to 10, then release them completely. Do the same for the muscles in your upper arms, forearms, hands, shoulders, chest, abdomen, thighs, lower legs and feet. Take your time.

4   When you're completely relaxed, imagine that you hear the sound of surf breaking on a beach. Better still, tape or buy a cassette of the sound of waves, and play it while doing the exercise.

EXERCISE: VISUALISATION

What is visualisation? The term may seem mysterious, but all it means is the ability to dream while awake.

Everyone visualises. At each stage in our lives, we dream that our desires will come true, we imagine ourselves in such and such a situation. In fact, we visualise almost constantly.

Start using this extraordinary capacity to your advantage. For example, use it as a means to relax.

1. Get comfortable in a quiet place, indoors or outdoors as you prefer. Sit or stretch out comfortably. Close your eyes.

2. Empty your mind for a few minutes. Watch the thoughts and ideas flowing through your mind, without trying to stop them.

3. Next, imagine a landscape that you like: a little country road bordered by flowers, a mountain path, a sandy beach, etc. See yourself walking through this landscape.

4. Try to distinguish as many details as possible about the landscape you're in — all the colours and shades of your surroundings.

5. Listen for sounds — insects, birds singing, trees rustling, waves crashing, etc.

6. Smell the odours of nature all around you. Breathe deeply. Feel the heat of the sun on your back. Enjoy the magic moment.

7. Stop the exercise wherever you wish. But don't get up right away. If your visualisation was effective, you'll need a few minutes to come back to reality. Just rest awhile, with your eyes closed. This will avoid any unpleasant feelings of temporary disorientation.

EXERCISE: CREATE A MENTAL OASIS

Numerous studies on the benefits of visualisation have pointed to the importance of creating your own mental oasis — a refuge fashioned according to your tastes, where you can go and spend a few minutes whenever you feel the need to relax or cool down, at any time during the day or night.

Here's how to create your place of mental retreat:

1   Get comfortable in a quiet place and close your eyes.

2   Imagine a place you consider idyllic, a place where you'd like to spend a long time. It could be a room that you've furnished and decorated; it could be a little clearing in the forest; a babbling brook lined with cedars; a mountain refuge; a mediaeval monastery; a cave with a floor of fine sand; an English or Japanese garden — the possibilities are endless.

    You can either completely invent your refuge, or visualise a place that exists already that you've come across on your travels. Let your imagination guide you.

3   Carefully examine your oasis. Smell all the odours, listen to the sounds. It should become as familiar to you as your bedroom. You may, from time to time, alter the décor if you so desire. Everything is permissible where imagination is concerned.

4   Retreat to your mental oasis at least once a day. It will be your secret garden, the place where you can get rid of all your cares, all your negative emotions and frustrations. You can go there to solve a problem that has been bothering you, or to think about things, or just to do your relaxation exercises.

2 Physical exercise
'Not again!' you say. Well, you must realize that because it

improves your physical and mental well-being, and instils a sense of confidence in yourself and in your image, exercise is an essential tool for mastering your emotions.

By exercising regularly, you combat tendencies like excessive perspiring, blushing, trembling and explosive anger, without even being aware of it.

Take a moment to look at some photographs of successful people in magazine ads. You'll quickly realize that an image of success is also one of physical well-being, which creates an impression of serenity in the face of life's trials and tribulations.

So what are you waiting for?

Although all forms of sport are beneficial, some are better suited to people who want to improve their emotional balance. These are endurance sports and martial arts. The former allow you to exteriorize your tensions and frustrations in a harmless way, while strengthening your body and improving your general mental and physical health. Martial arts improve your capacity to concentrate, which is the third prerequisite for emotional stability, as you'll see in the next section.

3 Learn how to concentrate

Have you ever tried to have a coherent conversation with someone who is overcome by emotion?

If so, you probably gave it up rather quickly. People who allow themselves to be entirely dominated by their emotions, who are prey to stress and nervous tension, are incapable of giving you their complete attention. You get the feeling you're talking to a wall.

When you're in a highly emotional state, your thoughts wander. You stammer and stutter, say almost anything that comes into your head, gesticulate excessively, and so on.

If you've succeeded, by applying the techniques outlined in the preceding chapters, in forming a positive image of yourself, it will be much easier for you to deal with other people. You'll be less intimidated, and you'll be able to concentrate not on what other people may be thinking about you, but on the subject of conversation.

How can you learn to concentrate? It's simple — just do daily concentration exercises.

There are thousands of kinds of concentration exercises. Most popular among them are crossword puzzles, mystery word games, and indeed puzzles of all sorts. But if you want to improve your concentration, or to be able to concentrate for a given period, then you have to time yourself. For example, give yourself 20 minutes to work on a series of problems, or one hour to complete a crossword puzzle, and so on. Because if you forget to time yourself, there's nothing to prevent you from letting your attention wander as often as you wish.

Here are a few suggestions for exercising your concentration.

EXERCISE: THE SPIRAL

On a white sheet of paper draw a spiral which is as uniform as possible. Fill the whole sheet of paper. Don't kid yourself — drawing a perfect spiral requires a lot of concentration.

EXERCISE: COUNTING

When you find yourself in a waiting-room at the doctor's or dentist's office, or waiting for a flight or train, amuse yourself by counting the squares on the floor or ceiling, or follow the pattern of the wallpaper with your eye. You'll improve your concentration, and the wait will seem a lot shorter. In fact, all exercises which require concentrating on a fixed point for any length of time are effective.

EXERCISE: CLOUDS

1 On a warm day, stretch out on the grass or on a beach or a lawnchair in your back garden and look at the clouds.

2 Try to pick out objects, animals or people in the moving spectacle above you. Keep doing the exercise for as long as you like. It's an excellent way to improve your powers of concentration, and it's so pleasant!

4 Get into the habit of analysing your emotional reactions

Each night before going to sleep, review any events that happened during the course of the day which produced some kind of emotional shock. Recreate each event in your mind, and try to imagine yourself undisturbed. You'll soon notice that you react less violently to similar events — in other words you'll become less emotional.

By analysing your emotions, you take the drama out of them. This is exactly the same process you employed to deal with your shyness. Without blaming yourself at all, you learn to judge how you should have reacted in a given situation. And soon you start reacting that way when a similar situation arises. This represents a huge step forward on the path to mastering your emotions.

LEARN SYSTEMATIC DESENSITIZATION

What does this consist of? Systematic desensitization helps you gain more control over yourself by removing certain sensory perceptions. The state is temporary, and purely physical, and will in no way affect your overall sensitivity.

1 How to desensitize your hearing

1 Make a list of all the noises that disturb you, make you

nervous, or produce some kind of emotional reaction (someone's voice, the noise made by certain household appliances, slamming doors, some types of telephone ringing, motorcycles in the street, etc.)

We all have to put up with noises that bother us. You'll soon find yourself with quite an extensive list. Don't hurry — take a few days to compile your list, if necessary.

2 Then, the next time you hear one of these sounds, repeat to yourself, 'I am calm, nothing can disturb my calm.'

3 Force yourself not to react to the noise — no gestures or nervous movements.

'Impossible!' you say. Not at all. To the human mind, nothing is impossible! It can adapt to any situation. You may know someone who lives close to a motorway or a railway line or a fast-running river. These people, after a short period of adaptation, stop hearing the noise from outside almost completely, and are surprised when guests complain they weren't able to sleep a wink all night because of it.

If you succeed in systematically desensitizing your hearing, you'll be able to concentrate and work in the midst of any noisy commotion. You'll also sleep better and calm your nerves somewhat. Try it! You won't be disappointed.

2 How to desensitize your vision

You wouldn't be human if you weren't susceptible to emotional shock through the things you see. It might be blood, a horror film, certain animals (reptiles apparently top the list, followed closely by spiders), even certain inert substances.

But it is possible to look at anything without becoming emotionally involved. How? In much the same way that you desensitized your hearing.

1 Start by making a list of visual images that provoke an emotional response in you.

2 Every morning in the shower, call one of those images to mind — an image that you actually can't stand to see. Imagine it in as much detail as possible, and repeat to yourself, 'I am calm, I feel nothing at all.'

3 Repeat the exercise until you've completely eliminated the emotional response from your system. Don't be discouraged if progress comes slowly. It's normal. Persevere!

3 How to deal with other people's emotions

Not only do we have a hard time dealing with our own emotions, we regularly have to deal with other people's as well! Think about it for a moment.

One of the characteristics of a charismatic personality is the ability to differentiate instinctively between one's own and other people's emotions. That's why such people seem so solid and self-assured, ready to face adversity calmly.

Your boss has an anxiety attack when a job becomes urgent, your spouse is angry because his or her squash partner cancelled, your mother rails about your father's laziness, and so on. Do any of these situations sound familiar?

Instead of aggravating your boss's anxiety or your spouse's anger or your mother's dissatisfaction, let them express their emotions. Don't get involved. You may, of course, express your compassion and sympathy. *But don't make their problem your problem.*

Repeat silently to yourself, 'This has nothing to do with me, it's not my problem, I'm not going to get involved.'

HOW TO ELIMINATE SYMPTOMS OF STAGE FRIGHT

This section is important. You are finally going to learn how to tame the demon that's been trailing you your whole life, preventing you from accomplishing what you dreamed of doing — being a performer, a statesman or an artist.

Everything you've learned in this book up to now will help you eliminate your stage fright. Through the combination of acquiring more self-confidence, improving your physical and psychological balance, learning to relax and desensitizing yourself so that you are not imprisoned by your emotions, you can also eliminate stage fright from your life.

Yoga and meditation are remedies for many types of problems, notably stage fright. Breathing exercises will also be very useful for overcoming stage fright and for preventing habitual blushing and stammering.

To get rid of recurring stage fright you can use three exercises: two before the event, and one during the event. The first two may be sufficient, but if not, use the third as well.

PREPARATORY EXERCISE: BREATHING

First calm yourself with this breathing exercise:

1   Breathe in deeply from the abdomen, counting to five, and repeating the syllables, 'I — am — fee — ling — calm.'

2   Hold your breath for five counts and repeat, 'I — am — fee — ling — calm.'

3   Breathe out completely, once again repeating, 'I — am — fee — ling — calm.'

PREPARATORY EXERCISE: VISUALISATION

1   Find a spot where you won't be disturbed for a few minutes and close your eyes.

2   Now imagine yourself in the situation that is about to take

place. For example, if it's a job interview, imagine yourself conversing calmly with the interviewer. Visualize yourself convincing him or her that you're right for the job. If you're going to take an oral exam, imagine yourself graciously receiving the applause of the audience. And so on.

3 Take a few deep breaths before opening your eyes again. A profound sense of well-being will pervade your mind and body.

EXERCISE: DURING THE EVENT

Actually, this part consists of a number of little tricks rather than an exercise *per se*. They make use of your sense of humour.

- Imagine the other person (or persons) who intimidate you so much in an inferior position, or one that is simply ridiculous. For example: if the person is very serious and strict, imagine him/her dressed as a clown or an angel.
- If the person is proud and overbearing, imagine them with their fly open, or in pyjamas, or in their underwear.
- If the other person intimidates you through arrogance, don't hesitate to apply a more aggressive technique. Concentrate for a few seconds on a precise point on the clothing of the other person — the lapel of a jacket, or the knot of a tie, or an earring. The person will start wondering whether something is wrong with the way they're dressed, and will almost certainly feel disconcerted. Take advantage of the moment to regain your cool!

Above all, follow this practical advice:

- Do not take any drugs to calm yourself down — no tranquillizers, no sleeping pills. If you're really worried about getting overexcited, take two aspirins, or a

homoeopathic remedy, and make yourself a cup of calming herb tea.
- Eat lightly, and avoid heavy meals which are difficult to digest.
- Don't drink alcohol, under the pretext that it will calm your nerves. The 'courage' it gives you is a complete illusion. Never forget that!
- Do physical exercise to improve your sleep. You'll need all you can get!
- Dress comfortably. Don't add to the stress of the moment by wearing a skirt or trousers that constrict your abdomen or waist, a collar that pinches your neck, tight sleeves that might tear if you move too suddenly, or shoes that pinch your feet.
- Choose familiar clothing that you feel comfortable in, and that you've already worn a number of times. If you absolutely insist on dressing up in something new, wear your outfit at home for a few hours each day and get used to how it feels.
- Don't dress too warmly. You'll be warm enough when the moment of truth arrives!
- And, of course, there's nothing like being well prepared for the event. If you know your subject well, the examiner will seem a lot less frightening; if you're sure of your qualifications for a job, it will be a lot harder for an interviewer to find fault with you . . . and so on.

If you do suffer from stage fright, don't blame yourself or say something like, 'I get stage fright, it's not my fault, there's nothing I can do about it.' Hundreds of famous people have been prey to terrible bouts of stage fright at different periods in their careers. But it didn't prevent them from attaining success.

SUMMARY

This chapter was about mastering emotions, a fundamental aspect of the fight against shyness. To acquire the assurance you lack, learn to master your emotions.

By completing a test, you got to know your emotional profile. Then you learned the four golden rules for mastering emotion: relaxation, exercise, concentration and analysis of emotional reactions.

In addition, the method of systematic desensitization helps you eliminate exaggerated reactions to external stimuli which usually bother you — unpleasant things you hear and see. You also learned that it's important to differentiate between your own emotions and those of others.

Finally, you were shown how to overcome stage fright, by following some practical advice and doing a few exercises both before and during an event that you're apprehensive about.

If you succeed in overcoming your emotional instability, you'll regain your lost credibility with the people around you. People who shout a lot are usually not heard! On the other hand, if you react calmly to stressful, tiring, unpleasant or even frightening situations, people will see you as someone who always knows how to take control and do the right thing. When you have something to say, people will listen.

CHAPTER EIGHT

How to Win the Confidence of Others

Are people you admire — people who have charisma — often late with their work? Do they wait for the phone company to disconnect the line before paying the bill? Are they often late for meetings? Do they leave a lot of dirty dishes around?

No. People with charisma — and we'd all like to be one of them — are never careless, under any circumstances. This is partly what inspires their confidence, and makes them appreciated. They're faithful, you can count on them. They respect their engagements, however minor they may be. They know that punctuality is, and always will be, a royal mark of respect.

They also know how to make rapid decisions, without hesitating too much. When they're asked to do a favour for someone, or when someone asks them a question, they don't hem and haw for hours before answering. How comforting it is to deal with people who know what they want — and what they don't want!

When an emergency arises, they know exactly what to do. They don't panic, they don't act precipitously — they think for a few moments and then act, calmly and effectively.

This chapter covers two further qualities, both of which you must acquire — if you don't already have them — in order to 'round off' your magnetic personality. They are the ability to make the right decision fast, and the habit of getting things done — i.e. not putting off until tomorrow what can be done today.

How to Win the Confidence of Others

1 LEARN TO REACT QUICKLY AND EFFECTIVELY

It's not all that difficult, as you'll soon see. But you can be sure that in our fast-moving and merciless world, the people whose minds work quickest usually come out on top. If you want to be listened to, respected and admired, you must be able to make the right decision, fast.

To find out about your own decision-making habits, do the following test. It was designed by psychologists, so even if some of the questions seem inappropriate, rest assured they're included for a reason.

TEST: DO YOU KNOW HOW TO MAKE FAST DECISIONS?

Answer these seven questions in 10 minutes or less:

1 You're in a train compartment. One of your travelling companions suddenly seems to be ill. What do you do?
   a) *You pull the emergency cord*
   b) *You let the train continue, and look for a conductor*
   c) *You let the train continue, and look for a doctor*

2 You walk into a room and see a child standing on the windowsill. What do you do?
   a) *You call the child softly*
   b) *You rush forward and take the child in your arms*
   c) *You try to get close as possible without disturbing the child*

3 Which of these five words is different from the others?
   - form
   - bed
   - policeman
   - sign
   - trade

4   Imagine that you're hoarding something. What would you prefer to hoard?
    a) *A million dollars in cash*
    b) *A million dollars in diamonds*
    c) *A million dollars in gold*

5   You ride by on your bicycle just as four bank robbers jump into their getaway car. You notice that one of the car's tyres is flat, and there's a good chance you could keep up on your bike. What do you do?
    a) *You immediately give chase*
    b) *You stop a car and ask the driver to follow the thieves*
    c) *You make a note of the car's licence plate, pedal to the nearest phone booth and call the police*

6   You're marooned on a large desert island. What would you prefer having?
    a) *A hunting rifle, ammunition and a spade*
    b) *Enough canned food to last you for three years*
    c) *A small boat*

7   You pass by an electric train track and notice that someone is stuck on the track. What do you do?
    a) *You try to move the person*
    b) *You call the police and then run to stand near the person*
    c) *You call the railway company*

And now for the verdict! Give yourself three points for each correct answer.

1   The correct answer is **c**. If you pull the emergency cord right away, you'll stop the train even though there may be a doctor on the train or at the next station. As for the conductor, all he can do is look for a doctor among the passengers, which you can do faster yourself.

2   The correct answer is **a**. Either of the other two actions risks startling the child and causing it to fall.

3   The word 'policeman' is different from the others because it cannot be used to form part of another word, as the others can (plat-form, bed-side, stop-sign, free-trade).

4   The correct answer is **b**. It's best to collect diamonds because they're most likely to retain their value, and they're easy to transport and sell.

5   **c** is the correct response. What would you do if you caught the thieves? You'd probably get hurt, if not killed. The best thing is to notify the police immediately and give them the number of the licence plate.

6   The correct response is **a**. Armed with a gun, ammunition and a spade, you'd survive longer than on a finite supply of canned food. As for the boat, it's really the least practical solution. You'd be better off taking your chances on the island and waiting to be rescued.

7   **b** is the correct answer. If you try to move the person you'll probably get electrocuted yourself. The best thing is to call the police (who will in turn get through to the railway company and the hospital) and then stand beside the person to stop any passing trains.

If you scored between 15 and 21 points:
Your mental agility is surprisingly good.

You know how to make the right decisions fast, and you are not likely to procrastinate or to act impulsively without thinking. You know that, whatever happens, it's better to think for a few seconds before acting. People undoubtedly consider you a person who knows what you're doing, and often turn to you for help.

If you scored between 9 and 12 points:
You act correctly sometimes, but you tend to let yourself be guided by impulse. Your reflexes are certainly excellent, but you don't take the time to think before jumping in.

If you scored less than 9 points:
You have a lot of serious work to do. You're not using your mind as you should. You tend to hesitate, and then make a snap decision just to get it over with. You must take charge of yourself!

Start by carefully reading the questions and answers to the test you've just completed over again. Make sure you understand why a reaction is the best thing to do in the given situation.

To learn how to act and react correctly at the right moment, it would be a good idea if you applied the following principles:

1 Train yourself under less stressful conditions
It's probably the stress of having to make a fast decision that causes you to lose part of your intellectual capacity. It takes too much of an effort to make the right decision, and the result is a veritable mental block. Start by doing the following exercise regularly.

EXERCISE: CRISIS SITUATIONS

1. Imagine a number of crisis situations that you're likely to have to face one day. For example, if you're a doctor, imagine that you're called to the bedside of a very sick person. If you're a student, imagine that during a course the professor asks you a point-blank question. And so on . . .

2. Think for a few seconds, then decide how you're going to react. Write your decision down on a piece of paper, and forget the exercise until the next day.

3. Next day, resume the exercise by using the same situations. What would your reactions be now? If you changed your mind from one day to the next, then your reactions leave something to be desired. Keep on training. You should notice a significant improvement in a few days. Then, when

a situation really does arise that calls for fast and decisive action, you won't be afraid because you'll have trained yourself for the occasion.

2 Never forget your objective

This may seem obvious, but it isn't. Our fast-paced lifestyle often makes it difficult to keep our objectives in mind. We have a thousand things to think about, so when we have to make an important decision we often act on the spur of the moment. Each night before going to sleep, think about your objectives, and about what you did during the course of the day to attain them. You can also write your thoughts down in a journal, or discuss them with your spouse or with a close friend.

3 Ask yourself what you have to lose

Psychological studies have shown that situations which disarm us sufficiently to prevent us from making the right decision are rarely life-and-death issues. Rather they are about opportunities to advance ourselves, to make some kind of progress, to affirm or improve ourselves.

Very few people are aware of the power of a simple change in attitude. If, when the time comes to make an important decision, you always succumb to panic and act rashly, you'll never stop blaming yourself for your own stupidity. On the other hand, if you tell yourself, 'I have nothing to lose and everything to gain,' you'll start thinking clearly, your mind will unblock, and you'll be lucid enough to make the right decision after a few moments of productive reflection.

Never forget that you alone control your destiny, and that it's up to you to make the decisions that will improve your life.

2 DON'T PUT THINGS OFF FOR LATER

Why do some people always seem to put things off for later? Even though they decide to do something, they just keep procrastinating, day after day. Their lives get bogged down in neglect and carelessness. Not only do they harm themselves, they harm others as well.

What such people have in common is a feeling of inferiority coupled with a strong dose of hostility towards others. For example, someone who always puts off studying material that is essential for an exam is unconsciously obeying a message which says that he or she won't pass the exam anyway, so why bother? It's not worth the trouble. Or if your procrastination usually takes the form of being late, it's probably because you unconsciously want to embarrass others by never being on time. And so on.

If you want people to admire your personality, you must rid yourself of this detestable habit. You must become punctual, efficient and responsible!

How to become punctual, efficient and responsible

Well, you're obviously not going to break a lifetime of bad habits in two or three days. But if you've decided, and really desire from the bottom of your heart, to be liked and appreciated by others, then you'll make the necessary effort.

You have to want it. No one can do it for you.

First of all, you have to understand why you always tend to put things off. Then, if you do your best to improve your self-image by following the advice in this book, you'll soon notice that your bad habits tend to dissolve. You'll feel more inclined to act, and you won't get the impression that others take you for some kind of imbecile. You will have gained enough self-love and self-respect to take pleasure in impressing others with your efficiency.

Here are a few tricks that should make your job easier. They're very simple to put into practice, and work well together. So use a number of them at the same time.

1 Leave yourself written reminders
You make shopping lists, don't you? You note your

appointments in your diary? Do the same thing to eliminate your tendency to procrastinate.

Leave reminders for yourself all over the place. Use small notepads and write yourself messages like: 'I'm not going to let life pass me by'; 'The world belongs to those who know how to take it'; 'The early bird gets the worm' (people who procrastinate also tend to have trouble getting out of bed); 'I'm not going to be outdone by so and so'; and so on.

Another way to do this is to use symbols. Wind a string around your finger, or place a colourful sticker on an urgent file, for example.

2 Establish a plan of action
In the morning when you get up, make a list of what you should do during the day, and don't go to sleep before you finish! Be realistic, and don't bite off more than you can chew. But make sure you respect your programme.

You'll soon find out that there's no more pleasant and gratifying sensation than going to bed at night knowing you've accomplished what you set out to do!

3 Proceed in stages
If you're a serious procrastinator, you'd better not try to do too much at once, because you won't get very far. Draw up a realistic list of the steps you could take.

For example, if you have to write a long report, start by writing one or two pages a day. If you have to do a complete housecleaning, do one room at a time, and so on. Use your convalescent willpower carefully.

4 Ride the impetus
Say you've finished a task — take advantage of the impetus it gives you to start another as soon as you finish, before inertia has a chance to slow you down again.

5 Improvise
If you suddenly remember something you should do — do it!

Don't wait! Get out the documents or materials you need and get to work. This is an excellent habit to develop.

For example, answer letters as soon as you get them. Pay your bills as soon as they come in. If someone gives you a job, start it immediately, and then get back to it whenever you can.

6 Set up a schedule

If you have trouble organizing your life, draw up a precise and, above all, a realistic schedule. For example, if you schedule a few minutes of physical exercise when you get up, you'll soon get into the habit, and find yourself doing it without thinking.

What you're trying to establish is a daily routine, where every important activity has its place.

7 Modify your environment

It's possible that your place of work or study is contributing to your tendency to procrastinate. Although some people can concentrate on their work in any environment, it is better to get rid of any distracting elements. For example, instead of studying for exams in a room equipped with a television or a stereo, you'd be better off working in a quiet corner of the university library. If your desk faces a window, move it — you'll be less inclined to watch the people in the street and get down to work.

The colours of our environment have an astonishing impact on our productivity. It has been shown, for example, that colours like green, turquoise, sky blue and grey improve concentration, both intellectual and manual. On the other hand, colours like pink, orange, apricot, pale yellow and beige are conducive to relaxation and rest.

Try to determine which type of atmosphere suits you best, and makes you more productive.

8 Differentiate between your tendency to procrastinate and circumstances which are beyond your control

There are occasions when you really have to put something off for later, for quite legitimate reasons. But if you're in the habit of procrastinating, you probably have trouble telling the difference. So make a list of things you have to do. Analyse each section. Write down your reasons for not completing the task. Is it legitimate? Can you get rid of whatever is holding you up, or is it completely out of your control?

This is very important. You'll probably discover that you've been fooling yourself for years about why you put things off.

9 Talk to a friend
It's likely that your bad habits have led in the past to confrontations with people who have become your involuntary victims. They know your habits, probably better than you think.

Talk to someone who likes you and knows you well. Ask them to watch your progress. If you weaken, they can help get you back on the right track more easily than you could yourself.

SUMMARY

Two personality traits characterize what are termed 'charismatic' persons: the ability to act quickly at the right time, and the faculty of not procrastinating.

Start training yourself by imagining relatively harmless situations where you have to make a decision. If you get used to making fast decisions under unstressful conditions, you'll have no more problems making the right decision in a crisis.

Next, don't lose sight of your objectives.

Finally, stay calm by learning to undramatize the situation. You'll be more lucid if you stay calm than if you get excited.

Follow the advice in this chapter. Be methodical in developing a programme of rehabilitation for yourself. Don't let yourself fall back into the trap of procrastination.

Tell yourself that your bad habits are depriving you of the success you deserve. In addition, they have certainly distanced many people, who have formed an image of you as someone who can't be counted on, and who is rarely on time.

It's up to you to change that negative image. You can if you want to!

CHAPTER NINE

How to Find – and Keep – Your Ideal Partner

THE BEGINNING OF A LOVING RELATIONSHIP

Why are some people called irresistible? Why do love and friendship come so easily to these people? What do they have that others don't?

They project positive vibrations. They have a sense of humour, they don't take themselves too seriously, and they are capable of sincere and spontaneous compassion. They are tactful, and considerate of others. Their warm nature tells other people that they care about and like them, and savour their company.

All this isn't as easy to do as it seems at first glance. Why? You'll understand in a moment.

HANDICAPS WHICH PROMOTE SHYNESS

1 Fear of rejection
If you're extremely shy, then you're probably a solitary person, or at least more solitary than you'd like. Shy people who lock themselves away in an ivory tower don't seem to care much about others. They enclose themselves in a bitter shell of delusion, deception and even hatred, which they sometimes can't prevent from showing when they get close to someone. They are often on the defensive, and always look for signs of rejection in other people.

If you have a negative self-image, if you don't like yourself, then you'll have trouble accepting the fact that others can like you, despite wishing desperately to win their affection.

In other words, you're very hard to please! You probably feel that no one is good enough for you.

Isn't this contradictory? Not at all, since this aspect of your problem is only a reflection of your ingrained insecurity. Your subconscious reasoning goes as follows: 'After all, if I'm hard enough to get along with, I'll never meet my soul mate, and I won't run the risk of being rejected.'

Simple, isn't it?

Which brings us to the second handicap which promotes shyness.

2 The desire to find the perfect partner

If you've been alone for a long time, it's probably because you've created an image of your perfect partner. Unfortunately, people are made of flesh and blood, and are never as beautiful, as intelligent, as sensitive, or whatever, as this image of perfection you carry around. So no one is able to please you.

This doesn't mean that you should throw yourself into the arms of the first person who comes along, whatever they happen to be like!

It's perfectly normal to seek out people with whom we feel an affinity, who have the same outlook towards life, the same interests, the same tastes, and so on. But you can be sure that if you expect too much from another person, then you're bound to be sadly deceived in your relationship, because no one will be able to live up to your ideal image. Then, instead of finding yourself in an exciting, passionate relationship, you become critical, moody and incapable of feeling satisfied.

In conclusion, you should understand that what you're doing by being excessively hard to please is simply looking for self-love in the guise of another person — you want to find someone who has all the positive qualities that you lack.

Does this seem like a good thing to do?

HOW TO CHANGE YOUR ATTITUDE

Use your head, and adapt the cost—benefit exercise described in chapter 4 on shyness to resolve this type of situation.

For example, look at one of your negative ideas concerning personal relationships. According to researchers who specialize in solitude, one of the most common ideas can be formulated as follows:

'There's no point in getting involved with someone who doesn't meet my standards.'

Let's use this statement as an example.

Negative idea: There's no point in getting involved with someone who doesn't meet my standards.

Advantages of this conviction:
1. By being hard to please, I won't be obliged to get involved with someone who doesn't live up to my expectations.
2. I avoid the anxieties of making contact and starting a relationship, because I don't see anyone around who's good enough for me.

25%

Disadvantages of this conviction:
1. I don't go out much.
2. I often long for companionship.
3. I may never meet the person who's good enough for me.
4. I'll stay single all my life.

75%

Positive idea: It would be better for me to express an interest in people, and start going out, even if they don't live up to all my expectations. Then, once I've acquired more self-assurance, I can be a little more choosy.

Advantages:
1. I won't be as lonely.

2 I'll acquire self-assurance, and I'll have less fear of being rejected.
3 I'll gradually learn what I like and don't like about myself. Then I can try to change and improve myself.
4 Other people will appreciate my company and become closer.

75%

Disadvantages:
1 I run the risk of being rejected at some time or other.
2 I expose myself to emotional hurt by lowering my defences.

25%

The first step is always the hardest

Another proverb which is as true today as it was 2000 years ago! The first step is always the hardest to take, especially for shy people. They lack that easy-going nature which would allow them to show a casual interest in someone. They try to escape, because they're afraid of looking silly. So what can they do?

Certain behavioural norms are almost universal. For example, specialists in human contact agree that the first three minutes of contact is decisive. Let's say someone introduces you to a person of the opposite sex at a party. You shake hands, or just say something like, 'Pleased to meet you.' But at the same time, you make a lightning-fast judgment about that person, and they do the same about you. And in the three minutes that follow, both your subconscious, and that of the other person, will decide the fate of that relationship.

Suppose the impression is mutually favourable. You now have to follow up on your advantage. What should you do to begin a pleasant conversation?

Three subjects of conversation: which to choose?

You have the choice of three subjects:
- the situation
- the other person
- yourself

1 The situation

This is usually the wisest choice. By starting a conversation about the situation both you and the other person are in at the moment, you place yourself on neutral ground. You demand nothing, you don't run the risk of scaring the other person off by being too personal. The ice is broken, with no commitment on either side.

2 The other person

Most people like to talk about themselves, and are happy to answer questions or respond to comments. However, if the other person is as shy as you are, then you have to be very tactful and avoid intimidating them with your first question. So it's usually better to stick to a neutral subject at first (the situation, mutual friends, events in the news, etc.) before getting on to more personal subjects.

3 Yourself

Starting a conversation by talking about yourself is the worst mistake you can make! It doesn't require much insight to realize that this is a favourite topic of solitary people. If you fall into that category, take care!

Psychologists have noticed that it isn't necessary to say anything particularly intelligent or stimulating to break the ice with someone. On the contrary!

A specialist on shy behaviour recounts the story of how, in his younger days, he approached a female student whom he found very attractive, by stammering: 'Your blouse is very pretty. It suits you.' As he finished speaking, he suddenly realized that the girl wasn't wearing a blouse, but an old, rumpled T-shirt! He felt the urge to panic, and blushed all the colours of the rainbow. His legs trembled. But he was even more surprised when the girl burst out laughing, put her arm through his and asked him his name.

Three ways to begin a conversation

There are three ways to begin a conversation, once you've decided what to talk about:

- ask a question
- express an opinion
- state a fact

The first two are the most effective. If you ask a question, any polite person will respond, and that will get the conversation rolling.

If you express an opinion, make it a positive one. For example, if you're at a party and start a conversation by saying something like, 'I can't stand all this cigarette smoke,' then you shouldn't be too surprised if the other person responds by saying, 'Then why don't you leave?' Instead you should say something like, 'The atmosphere here is great, isn't it?' or 'This party was a great idea!'

The possibilities are infinite.

You can state a fact as a last resort, but you run the risk of getting into a boring conversation. It's better to engage the attention of the other person immediately by asking a question or expressing a positive opinion. Things will go a lot more smoothly than if you say something like, 'It's raining this evening,' or 'I was late getting here.'

How to formulate an invitation

The ice is broken, you've discovered some common interests. Now you'd like to continue the relationship by extending an invitation.

Note: all the information in this chapter, as well as in the rest of the book, applies to women as well as to men. Times have changed, and women don't have to stand around and wait, eyes lowered, for a man to invite them to dance, or take a walk around the garden and look at the stars. So if you're a woman, don't tell yourself, 'I have to leave it up to him to start a conversation. After all, that's what he's supposed to do. If he doesn't say anything, it means he doesn't find me attractive.'

That would be a terrible mistake!

If you're sure you felt something when you first made eye contact, then it's as much up to you as to the man to start a conversation, or to extend an invitation to carry on the relationship and see each other again. By finally acquiring their rights, women have also assumed the responsibilities that go along with those rights. There are no two ways about it!

Now back to the invitation — here is some advice you can follow:

- Start by learning about the interests of the other person. If you're told that he or she gets seasick, then it wouldn't be a good idea to extend an invitation to go sailing!
- Be direct. For example, don't start by vaguely asking, 'Are you doing anything next Saturday night?' The majority of people would be:

  1 Embarrassed at having to say, 'No, I'm not doing anything.'
  2 Put off by the idea of either having to lie or accept your invitation, rather than telling you they'd rather stay home than go out with you.

  A better, more direct approach would be simply to say: 'Would you like to have a drink/go sailing, etc. next Saturday?'
- Don't ask for too much right away — the other person will be more likely to accept an invitation to have a coffee with you in a few days, than to have dinner at your parents' house the following evening! Formulate an invitation that implies no commitment, and that's easy to accept. Be modest with your demands, at least at the outset.

Our attitude determines that of the other person

Pay attention to the way your attitude influences the way the other person will react: strangely enough, the way you behave has a strong influence on the way others register an invitation, even if they're not aware of it. Let's look at two examples — choose the invitation you'd prefer to accept:

1. The person casts furtive glances your way, crosses and uncrosses their arms and legs, and then says, very seriously:

    'I know you're probably very busy but . . . I'd really like to see you again. Maybe we can be friends. Would you like to play tennis on Saturday morning?'

2. The person looks you right in the eye and, smiling, says:

    'I'm happy we met, and I'd like to see you again. Why don't we get together for tennis — we can invite so-and-so and make it a party — on Saturday morning, if you're free.'

Obviously, 99.9 per cent of the population would be more likely to accept the second invitation. What about you? Well, the same goes for the invitations you extend — make it easy for the other person to accept.

What to do if you are refused

This doesn't mean the other person is rejecting you. He or she is simply rejecting your invitation. Maybe s/he'd like to see you but doesn't play tennis, or maybe s/he's just really busy at the time you suggest. If so, there's nothing simpler than suggesting another time.

On the other hand, your invitation may be refused with absolutely no explanation. Don't insist. The other person probably won't tell you the truth anyway, and insisting will just make the situation very unpleasant. Retreat graciously by saying something like, 'Too bad, I would have liked to get to know you.' You can also give the person your telephone number, and tell them to call if and when they're available.

Whatever happens, don't get depressed because you were refused. If you're sure the spark you felt on first contact is mutual, there's nothing to prevent you from persevering later on. But don't be indiscreet or impolite — you'll only turn the other person off.

HOW TO FEEL GOOD TOGETHER

A good image for a loving relationship is a scale. Each side does his or her part, places it on a tray and, after all is said and done, both trays should be equal.

How can this fragile equilibrium be maintained?

1 Let your relationship develop on its own

Don't rush things! If you feel good with someone, don't ruin it by asking for too much too soon.

If you start talking about marriage after a couple of weeks, if you leave your toothbrush in the other person's bathroom the first time you're invited over, if you want to go on vacation after knowing someone for three days, then you're heading for failure. By insisting on talking about the future while the present is uncertain, you destroy both the present and the future.

Don't make the mistake of discussing your relationship before a solid foundation has been established. It's the best way to scare someone off. Also remember that if you spend more time talking about the relationship than living it, it means the relationship is on the rocks, and the best thing may be to just end it.

2 The power of laughter

Laughter is one of the most marvellous gifts nature has given us. It protects us against disease, saves us from depression, and helps us survive extremely stressful situations without losing our minds completely. Laughter makes life worth living.

Laughing with your partner is a way of getting close to him or her, of being in harmony by thinking on the same wavelength. Shared laughter becomes a happy memory.

We can be attracted to people because they make us laugh.

Cultivate your sense of humour — people will appreciate you all the more for it. If you exude happiness and well-being, people will enjoy your company.

Laughing is an excellent way to get close to people. When we laugh together, we become accomplices, a bond is formed between us which can overcome any barrier. Don't take your relationships too seriously. Reserve a special place for laughter — and humour — in your life!

3 Know how to ask and offer

Don't think that you can attract love by not asking for anything, and by suppressing your deepest desires. You have a perfect right to want things, and to express what you want. You have the right to your opinions, and you should hope that people respect them.

Never tell your partner: 'It doesn't matter which film we see, as long as I'm with you.' Actually what you're saying is that you have no personality, and that you depend entirely on the other person to make the decision, which places an enormous weight on his or her shoulders — i.e. guessing, somehow, what would please you.

Neither should you be afraid to express your feelings. Don't give your partner the impression that, although you're together, you could be just as happy with someone else; it wouldn't make all that much difference! If you do, you are courting catastrophe. No one likes to be thought of as a substitute. On the contrary, we appreciate the love others have to give, and we feel happy when someone shows that they love us.

4 Whatever happens, maintain your dignity

If you tend to be shy, then you know how important a sense of dignity is. It is in large part a fear of losing your dignity that causes you to lead a solitary life in the first place.

To maintain your dignity within the context of a relationship, you have to be independent *before* getting involved. This may seem obvious. Yet how many people do you know who consider their relationship as a kind of life saver? Count them —

you'll be very surprised by the result.

This kind of relationship is bound for failure right from the start. No one can be for you what you don't have the courage to be for yourself. No one can be happy for you. Happiness is inside you! All you have to do is help it along. Your partner should not be a parent, or a child, or a crutch.

Don't believe the popular romantic myth which claims that when you love someone, you 'share everything'. Nothing could be further from the truth. Don't forget that you are a complete and whole individual. You've lived a lot of years before running into your soul mate. During those years you acquired a character, tastes and interests which are your own, not to mention your hereditary characteristics!

If you want your relationship to remain balanced, and to maintain your sense of dignity, don't forsake your personality, tastes and interests to satisfy the other person. He or she won't be grateful for it, and they may end up despising you for having so little backbone.

To conclude, here's a very interesting test. Use it to evaluate your own relationships. A detailed commentary on each question has been provided, as well as an overall evaluation. Whatever the results, if you modify your attitude in accordance with the advice, you'll feel your relationship take on new life. You can be sure of it!

It's up to you!

TEST: WHAT KIND OF PARTNER ARE YOU?

Answer yes or no to the following questions. Don't hesitate — answer quickly, honestly, and don't go back and change your responses. The authors of the test, psychologists, have deliberately omitted choices like maybe, sometimes, rarely, etc.

1   Objectively speaking, do you usually consider your partner to be a nice person?

2. Do you blame your partner for your failures?

3. Are you envious of your partner's success?

4. Do you expect your partner to instinctively know when you need tenderness?

5. Do you keep your suspicions to yourself?

6. Are you jealous of a friendly relationship your partner has with someone else?

7. Do you lose control when he or she is angry with you?

8. Do you make secret sacrifices for your partner?

9. Do you wash your dirty laundry in public (do you discuss private matters in public)?

10. Do you continue to do things your partner disapproves of?

11. Do you usually tolerate your partner's weaknesses?

12. Do you always do exactly what you want to do?

13. Do you always listen to your partner attentively?

14. When you're wrong, do you admit it?

15. Are you satisfied with your partner's professional accomplishments?

16. Do you get upset when he or she doesn't feel like making love?

17. Do you feel more responsible for your parents than for your partner?

18. Do you ask for your partner's help when necessary?

19. Can you accept being alone? Can you accept your partner's need to sometimes be alone?

20. Do you appreciate the leisure time you spend together?

Answers

1. Yes. It's much easier to live in harmony when you find someone is a nice person. You have to become friends before you can become lovers.

2. No. It's very difficult to live with someone who does not accept responsibility for his or her actions. By blaming someone else, you're just feeding your ego, and destroying that of the other person. This is not the best way to get someone to love you!

3. No. If you're successful in your own life then you'll have no reason to be jealous about your partner's success.

4. No. No one, not even the person closest to you, should have to guess your desires.

5. No. Suspicions can eat away at a couple's happiness, and eventually poison it beyond repair. Being frank should be one of your priorities. Discuss things with an open heart and mind.

6. No. Jealousy is a sign of insecurity. Try to rid your life as a couple of this destructive demon, which can destroy you both. Talk frankly and openly about your fears. Don't let them dominate you.

7. No. Try not to take what your partner says to heart when he or she is angry. In a couple, one person's anger is often the result of insecurity, and is used to try to blame the other person. Don't fall into the trap.

8. No. As we've already said, self-denial is not a particularly useful virtue in life. Martyrs have their place in the history books, but not in families. They are certainly hard to live with, and don't forget that it's often the victim who is really the executioner.

9. No! If you've read the book or seen the film *Who's Afraid Of Virginia Woolf*, forget about it! Discussing private matters

in public is one of the surest ways to get your partner to hate you. Doing so is a violation of your intimacy together, and a form of mental cruelty.

10 No. It's better to discuss an issue openly rather than antagonize your partner by continuing to do things he or she disapproves of.

11 Yes. If you reject your partner because of his or her weaknesses, it's probably because you feel emotionally insecure yourself. Try to help and understand your partner. You are not without your own weaknesses.

12 No. Living with someone should be a perpetual exchange. No one likes to give without receiving, and a person who always gets without giving ends up despising the giver.

13 Yes. There's nothing more exasperating than talking to a wall! If you want other people to like you, listen to them, whether it's your boss, your spouse or anyone else.

14 Yes. It's certainly much more pleasant to live with someone who admits when they're wrong, apologizes and learns from their mistakes.

15 Yes. It's not up to you to judge. If you're not satisfied with your partner's professional standing, it may be that your relationship is suffering from a problem that neither money nor social standing can solve.

16 No. We don't always experience the same desires at the same time. There's nothing personal about refusing to make love once in a while.

17 No. If you do, your relationship is in trouble. You don't live with your parents any more, but with your partner, and that's where your loyalty should lie. Don't compare your partner to your parents.

18 Yes. Remember that it's as difficult to live with someone who never needs help as it is to live with someone who is incapable of taking care of themselves.

19 Yes. The ability to take pleasure in a few moments of solitude is a sign of maturity, as is the ability to respect someone else's need to be alone from time to time.

20 Yes. Sharing leisure time remains one of the happiest memories of living as a couple.

Results

If you obtained between 5 and 10 correct responses:
You are a demanding partner, difficult to live with, and probably suspicious. It's likely that your deep sense of insecurity causes you to oppress the person you're with. Read this book over again from the beginning, and try hard to improve your self-image. You can still save your relationship!

If you obtained between 11 and 14 correct responses:
You may be very difficult to live with, but in general you do know how to get along with your partner. You're certainly a troubling kind of person — people say it's hard to get to know you. You can improve your relationship by learning to be more flexible.

If you obtained between 15 and 19 correct responses:
Your partner is very lucky to be sharing such a balanced relationship. You're not overly demanding, but you don't let anyone walk all over you either. You know how to preserve your self-respect and dignity, but you know how to give love as well.

If you had 20 correct responses:
Do the test again! If you score 20 out of 20 again, then you're that rare jewel — the ideal partner everyone dreams of having! You probably have to refuse a marriage proposal every week! Lucky you.

SUMMARY

If you're looking for a loving relationship, excessive shyness can be a serious handicap. But if you've been applying the advice contained in this book from the start, then you're on the threshold of eliminating it.

To be loved, you have to love.

Fight the negative thought patterns that are condemning you to a life of solitude! You reject all your potential partners because you are afraid of being rejected yourself. You look for a perfect mate because deep down you know that person doesn't exist.

To make initial contact easier, read over the advice in this chapter from time to time.

Once your relationship has started, you have to nurture it so it doesn't wither and die.

A relationship is exactly like a physical body. It's hard to make it look perfect, but as soon as you stop caring for it, it deteriorates in less time than it takes to tie your shoes. On the other hand, the stronger it is, the faster it can regain its former vigour.

Nourish your relationship by insisting on certain key points: laughter, learning to ask and offer, preserving individual dignity and self-respect, and refusing to sacrifice your personality.

CHAPTER TEN

How to Become a Leader

If you have acquired an attractive and charismatic personality by applying this method, then you possess all the trump cards for becoming a leader. Play those cards!

Certain people have an innate sense of authority. Most historical figures who had charisma were leaders. The magnetism emanating from them attracted multitudes of supporters and disciples. This authority, this personal power, can be acquired methodically.

First let's see what the power you already have is like. Do the following test to determine whether or not you have the makings of a leader, as things stand at the moment.

TEST: DO YOU POSSESS LEADERSHIP QUALITIES?

1. Look at the three lines of numbers below. If you add them up to get three sums, which of these sums would be highest? (You have 10 seconds to answer — don't cheat!)
   a. 0 8 3 6 0 1 5 7
   b. 5 1 9 0 0 3 5 1 4 0
   c. 4 1 9 0 5 0 1 4

2. In general, people need to know why they are ordered to do something.
   True   False

3. You believe that there are times when your decisions should not be questioned.
   True   False

4   People who lead others should establish personal relations with those they lead.
    True   False

5   To create an impression of objectivity, a boss should turn a deaf ear to the problems of his colleagues.
    True   False

6   In any cross-section of the population, some people are so weak or so stupid that they're never good for anything.
    True   False

7   Above all, a good leader must be feared.
    True   False

8   Asking advice from colleagues or family members is a sign of weakness.
    True   False

9   Praise is more productive than criticism.
    True   False

10 It's better to work day to day than to make long-range plans.
    True   False

11 A leader's emotions have little influence on the productivity of those around him/her.
    True   False

12 If we get angry with someone, we should show it and not restrain ourselves.
    True   False

13 A real boss should do the greatest part of the work himself.
    True   False

Answers
Give yourself 10 points for each correct answer.

How to Develop Charisma & Personal Magnetism

Question	Correct Answer
1	a
2	True
3	True
4	False
5	False
6	False
7	False
8	False
9	True
10	False
11	False
12	False
13	False

If you scored between 110 and 130 (the maximum) points:
You have the makings of a leader, at least if you answered the questions honestly. If you don't occupy a position of authority at present, it's probably because you never cared to, or because it simply doesn't interest you. That's unfortunate, because you'd make an excellent director. You have the talent and instinct for attaining personal power, and the good sense not to abuse it.

If you scored between 50 and 100 points:
You're certainly not a born leader, but you can easily become one by learning the appropriate techniques. For example, follow the method described in this chapter. You shouldn't have much trouble getting to the head of the class. All you need is a little discipline and perseverance.

If you scored 40 points or less:
You're doubtlessly a shy and introverted person, more comfortable surrounded by the books in your study than at the head of a hierarchy. But if you can overcome your shyness by applying the methods contained in this book, you may discover a hidden taste for authority in yourself. Even if this is not the

case, it's always useful to know how to steer the boat. You never know what situations life will throw your way.

WHAT CONSTITUTES THE PERSONAL POWER OF A REAL LEADER?

1 A real leader has no trouble rallying excellent supporters

A person who demonstrates real leadership qualities has no trouble procuring efficient support. Other people are willing to put themselves out for his or her sake, without even thinking about it. This is one of the characteristics of real personal power.

2 A real leader influences others

As your personal power develops, you influence others more easily. Even when you don't make any special efforts to convince them, people listen to you, follow your advice and try to imitate you.

3 A real leader knows how to manage his/her time

A real leader is someone who knows how to manage time, how to be perfectly organized, and who is always punctual. By respecting his own schedule, he also respects other people's.

4 A real leader knows how to sell

Making use of personal power means knowing how to convince people. Therefore, a good leader is also a good salesperson, capable of making any initiative look attractive, and of rallying people to his or her cause. A leader knows how to sell himself, and his ideas.

If you follow the method described in this chapter, you'll soon master these four abilities. But before developing your personal power, you must adopt an attitude that will automatically separate you from the mass of anonymous followers.

STEP 1: START BY REFUSING TO BE ANONYMOUS

If you want to profit from your leadership qualities, the first thing you have to do is emerge from the anonymous mass of your fellows. You have to be noticed and appreciated; your counsel, competence and special gifts should be sought out.

You should make your emergence gradual. Impose yourself through your qualities, not by stepping on people. Let others lift you above the mass, on their own initiative.

How?

There are a number of ways to go about it, depending on your lifestyle and the kind of work you do. You could also apply them all. The results will be all the more spectacular!

Acquire special skills

If you've been around the job market for a few years, then you know that these days, more than ever before, employers, whether in the private or public sector, are looking for candidates who are both multi-talented and specialized. Put into secular terms, this means they want icing on the cake!

It's up to you to give them what they're looking for!

Over and above your usual qualifications, which are probably fairly equal to those of a large number of other people, you should acquire some highly specialized skill, in a related field. Make it your personal pride. Read, study, take courses, keep yourself up to date. Never before in human history has it been so easy to acquire knowledge and skill, in whatever area. Take advantage of the opportunity.

The simple fact that you are continuing your education shows your employers that you're a dynamic person, always ready to develop your talents. And if you manage to acquire expertise in some rare but useful area, they'll be in seventh heaven! It won't be long before you're noticed, you can be sure of it.

So start looking around today for some area that you could specialize in. You'll add another string to your bow, while maintaining your present general level of competence. Not only will you be of greater use to your employers, you'll also be in a better position to find another job if, for one reason or another, you lose your present one.

You have everything to gain! Ask yourself now, 'Which area could I specialize in?' and 'How shall I go about it?'

Always be impeccably polite
It's a curious sign of the times that the simple fact of being polite is enough to get you noticed! Yet it's true. In this day and age where 'everything goes' people who practise good old courtesy are appreciated more than ever.

Being polite doesn't mean being spineless or hypocritical. On the contrary, courtesy is a manifestation of the respect you feel for others.

Thanking someone for services rendered (as minor as they may be), holding a door open for someone, smiling at a cashier, a mechanic or a porter, not interrupting someone — all these little actions serve to make life in society easier. Don't neglect them. They don't cost anything, and people appreciate them all the more today, since they've become so rare.

Be deferential towards others
Deference (acknowledging the authority of others) is also a forgotten virtue. If we meet someone who seems to be respectful, either on a personal or professional level, we immediately conclude that that person is servile and weak, or that he or she is only pretending in order to get something from us.

Get rid of that attitude! Show your respect to whomever you think merits it, whether because of their opinions, knowledge, qualifications or authority.

For example, if you have to call in the plumber, leave him alone to work in peace instead of hovering around like a mosquito. Respect his professional competence.

If someone expresses an opinion entirely contrary to your own during the course of a conversation, don't jump up and shout, 'That's totally ridiculous!' If you feel you absolutely must be heard, then calmly say something like, 'I can't say I share your opinion because . . .'

Learn how to captivate other people

To emerge from anonymity, you have to know how to arouse interest in the people around you. Actually, getting people interested isn't enough. If you really want to be a leader, you have to captivate people. Make them become immediately receptive to your personal power.

The best way to do this is through your eyes. Develop a striking gaze.

How do you react when someone stares at you?

- you don't even realize it
- you return the stare defiantly
- you become embarrassed
- you feel flattered

To captivate others, concentrate on the eyes. Don't feel flattered or embarrassed by someone's stare. Don't stare back. But show that you are aware of someone by shooting a flashing glance at them, right back in their eyes. The flash in your eyes should be the same as when you suddenly spot an old and dear friend in a crowd.

Don't grimace or smile — just look. The flash will register, and communicate that you acknowledge and recognize the person staring at you, even though you may not know them personally. To acknowledge someone by looking back at them is to captivate them.

In a world where indifference and the individual reign, this kind of contract sparks immediate interest in others. People feel they can approach you, and overcome the barriers that usually separates us. In other words, they become sensitive to your personal power.

STEP 2: LEARN TO LEAD

FIND EFFECTIVE SUPPORT

A leader is nothing without the collaboration of his or her

supporters. The team you gather around you is what makes you a real leader. You need effective and efficient support.

There are three main ways to gain support: through force, through trickery, or by deliberately inciting people to work with you. And, of course, the value of your support depends, above all, on your motives! Of course, the best support is the kind you obtain openly and deliberately, without force or trickery.

Nevertheless, all types of support have at least some value, as long as you recognize and use it for what it is. Don't be taken in by an offer of support. Try to detect the motive behind it, and if you think it's worthwhile, make use of it.

How can this be achieved on a day to day basis? Here's some practical advice.

SIX PRACTICAL POINTS FOR BEING A BETTER LEADER

1 Don't formulate orders in a tone of command

You know how you react to petty dictators? Well, keep in mind that other people don't like being bossed around any more than you do.

Get into the habit of formulating your orders as requests, or as joint decisions. Let's look at a few examples.

When talking to a subordinate, replace:

'I want this done by tomorrow morning.'
with
'You'd really be helping me out if you could get this done by tomorrow morning.'
or
'You'd be getting me out of a bind if you could . . . (and explain why).'

When talking to your children, replace:

'Clean up your room or you're not going out on Saturday!'
with
'Could you clean up your room a little before you go out? I'd appreciate it.'

However, don't forget that an order is still an order, no matter how it's packaged. And never give an order unless it's absolutely necessary. People will then take the order seriously, and be more likely to come through for you.

Similarly, avoid ultimatums as much as possible. There's hardly anything as degrading as feeling that you're subject to an ultimatum. Any support you gain in this way will be forced and involuntary, and you will elicit resentment since you are, in a sense, humiliating the person. Ultimatums should be used as a last resort. They are more in keeping with petty dictators than real leaders.

2 Use the 'we' technique

Try to replace 'you' with 'we' when issuing a command. In other words, instead of saying to your secretary:
'Mail this letter off today, please.'
you could say
'We have to get this letter off today. Could you take care of it?'

By replacing the imperative 'you' with 'we', you solicit the voluntary collaboration of the other person, based on your common interests. And, of course, this way of doing things is much more effective.

But, I hear you say, it isn't always possible to formulate instructions in this way. Well, that's true, but do it as often as possible, and you'll soon see how effective this apparently simple technique is.

Practise on your own. Write down the orders you usually have to issue to your family or at work.

Now reformulate them, using 'we' as much as possible. Practise saying them out loud. When the time comes to issue an order, try it. It'll sound completely natural.

3 A variation of this technique

Issue orders by asking questions:

'Don't you think we should do something to rectify the situation?'

'What if we did something about that door?'

These kinds of questions call for a decision. Other people are flattered that you respect them enough to ask for their opinion, and will be ready to do a lot more for you.

Practise formulating your commands in the form of questions, as you did with the 'we' technique. Practise them out loud, and make them sound natural.

4 Learn to delegate

One of the questions in the test you just did was about delegating. A real leader knows how to delegate. If you know you have efficient supporters, then you should have no trouble delegating.

An incredible number of managers complain that they can't delegate anything, even the simplest job. They feel they are indispensable for every little thing, and spend most of their time working. Why? Because they're doing their own work and the work of their subordinates as well.

How did they get into this kind of situation?

Well, instead of always commenting on the deficiencies of their employees, they should spend a little time thinking about their own defects as a leader. Because a bad leader never has good followers. Learn to trust your supporters.

Do the following exercise.

EXERCISE: JOB INVENTORY

---

1   List all the jobs you have to take care of every day.

   ● Check off the jobs that give you most satisfaction.

- Next, use another symbol or a colour to check off the jobs that seem most important, which you absolutely should take care of yourself.
- Next, check off the routine, ordinary jobs.

2 Now make a list of the people you work with. Besides their names, write what you consider to be their strong points, their speciality, and their main quality as a professional.

3 Now delegate your routine jobs as best you can, in a completely theoretical way. Divide the workload according to the respective characteristics of your co-workers.

4 Now calculate the percentage of time this theoretical delegating could save you, time you could use to do the really important or satisfying jobs. You'll be surprised by the result.

5 Put your theory into practice! If you've hardly delegated in the past, you can expect a little griping at first. But in a short time, you should see your employees overflowing with enthusiasm and good will — they will be pleased at finally being taken seriously and treated like the productive adults they are.

5 Learn how to praise others

This was also covered in the test. Remember your school years. Weren't you more motivated by praise and good marks than by criticism and blame?

We all like to feel appreciated. Don't hesitate to praise your supporters if they do their work well. Don't exaggerate in long-winded flattery — just let them know that you appreciate a job well done in simple and clear terms: 'The report you did last week was excellent,' or 'I really appreciate the effort you're making,' or 'I appreciate the work you're doing.' Be as precise as possible.

Even though they may have already been recompensed with overtime pay, your employees will appreciate being told personally and politely that you appreciate the work they're putting in.

And in future, you won't have any trouble finding volunteers to work overtime when the need arises.

6 Solve problems rapidly

Don't let embarrassing or problematical situations develop into crises. You'll be the first victim. Treat the abscess as soon as you know it's there!

If some of your subordinates seem unhappy or dissatisfied, be direct and simply ask them what the problem is. Don't overdramatize things — there's no need for a public confrontation. Just make it clear that you're available, and if they want to talk something over they're welcome.

If an employee walks around frowning all the time, ask discreetly if he still likes his work, if everything's all right at home, if his health is OK, etc. Let him know that you care. If he's having personal problems, he may open up and talk about them, and feel a lot better for it.

Don't ask questions behind the person's back. S/he certainly won't appreciate it if s/he finds out.

Be diplomatic. If the person isn't ready to talk, don't press the point. Just let him know that you hope his troubles will soon be solved, and that you're there if he needs you.

INFLUENCING OTHERS

In order to apply your personal power, you have to learn how to influence others, not to make them do harmful or unpleasant things, but simply to make them accept you as their natural leader.

A few simple techniques will help you get what you want from others. Their aim is to place another person in a flexible frame of mind, and make that person really want to satisfy you.

1 Don't hesitate to compliment people on the way they look

The simple fact of saying, 'You look great today!' has the effect of a magic potion on other people. We're all very conscious of our appearance. If someone compliments us on the way we look or dress, it brightens up our day.

And by praising your colleagues, or anyone you want to influence, on their appearance, you really do affect the way they look! If you say to someone, 'That jacket looks great on you!' then s/he will start thinking it looks great. And what is beauty but a subjective evaluation? This is how the psychology of persuasion works.

2 A powerful weapon: the art of listening

We've talked about this before: for other people to like you, to obtain what you desire, to be able to get shy people to come out of their shells, you have to know how to listen.

Most people like to talk about themselves, whether about their successes or problems. You'll build a reputation as a master conversationalist if you let other people talk about the books they're reading, the trips they've taken, childhood memories, professional accomplishments, and so on.

If a colleague or an employee wants to tell you about his or her problems, lend a sympathetic and attentive ear. If s/he asks for advice, make a few suggestions. But never, never talk about your own problems. The other person doesn't want to listen to you. But if you want to influence that person to do something for you, then listen to what they have to say.

Also, get into the habit of listening to people who can do a lot for you. The information they reveal may be very useful one day.

3 Know how to take criticism

Does this seem contradictory? Well, you'll see in a moment that it's entirely logical.

We've been encountering critics since childhood. In fact, there are many people who take a sadistic kind of pleasure in seeing others making mistakes, getting blamed, or making a fool of themselves in public.

If you feel people criticize you a lot, console yourself. There is a direct relation between how much you're criticized and how much you succeed! The higher you get, the more you'll be criticized.

By learning to accept criticism, you turn it to your advantage. In fact, it will help you extend your influence over others.

Here's some advice on how to take criticism:

- Look at criticism as proof of your progress. By progressing, you become a threat to others who are convinced they can never match your performance. This awareness should increase your self-confidence.
- Never fight with a critic. The spontaneous reaction to criticism would be a sharply worded retort. Control yourself!

If you're being criticized about your work, ask the person calmly to explain why he or she thinks that way. In a respectful and interested tone, ask just what it is he or she doesn't like about your work, and why. Then tell him or her how much you appreciate the observations and analysis. In this way you disarm your critic, who leaves with a feeling of having succeeded. The next time you ask that person for something, you can be sure s/he'll do all he can to help you.

If someone decides to criticize something about your personal life, or the way you dress, remain completely indifferent. The critic will tire of being ignored, and look for other prey.

4 Forget about personal vengeance
This is hard advice to follow. Yet how much human suffering is caused by a desire for vengeance!

The ancient Greek dramatists despised vengeance, and

portrayed it as a manifestation of the most terrible of crimes. We haven't made much progress since. On the contrary! Our society seems to applaud vengeance — if you don't believe it, just go to the cinema!

Even if someone does you wrong, don't waste your time and energy trying to get revenge. Sooner or later, those responsible will have to pay for their mistakes. Revenge brings us down to the level of those who create the problems in the first place. Don't give in!

An act of vengeance is usually much more apparent than the act which provoked it. If someone is out to harm you, s/he'd do it carefully, surreptitiously, and not out in the open. You're probably the only one who knows about it. If you're sure you're in the right and do decide to take revenge, you'll only be stirring up a lot more trouble. People will judge your action out of context, and blame you for it. This isn't the way to influence others! You'll be seen as a vindictive, unjust and petty person.

5 Avoid misplaced familiarity

Familiarity breeds contempt, as the saying goes. Although that may be a little extreme, you should be aware that you can exert more influence over people if you maintain a certain distance.

Always address your subordinates or colleagues with respect. Today, everyone starts calling you by your first name as soon as they meet you. This is especially true in the US, where sales techniques and the way people approach each other are much more informal than elsewhere in the world.

Let a little time go by before getting onto a first-name basis, especially with subordinates. And if you address people with respect, they'll soon realize where you're coming from, and do the same for you.

6 Manage your time

If you've learned to delegate effectively, then time is probably no longer a problem for you. But there are always crisis situations, both at work and at home, and it's always the people who know how to manage their time who come out on top.

What are the principles of effective time management?

Make a list of everything you have to do
Don't spend your days blindly jumping from one activity to another. Know exactly what you're going to do and how you're going to do it. Keep an agenda and note all your appointments, telephone calls, special tasks, etc.

When you complete a task, cross it off your list. You'll experience a pleasing sense of satisfaction.

Each night, take a look at the page for the following day. You'll wake up prepared for the new day.

If you weren't able to do everything you'd hoped one day, cross the items out and copy them onto the next day's page. But try to respect your schedule as much as possible.

Fight any tendency to procrastinate
A leader never puts things off. If he did, he'd never accomplish anything.

If you have even a slight tendency to procrastinate, read over the chapter covering this harmful habit and get rid of it.

Establish a list of priorities
You can't solve all your problems at once. Don't run around trying to do too much at the same time — you'll only end up doing very little.

Establish your priorities, and start with the top of the list. Don't worry about the other items for the moment — their time will come. Be methodical!

Don't let yourself be interrupted in the middle of an important task
This may seem obvious, but how many times a day are office workers distracted by colleagues who seem to have nothing better to do than spend their time chatting? Look around, and you'll soon realize that this is a serious problem.

Politely let people know that you won't be available for the next few hours, but that if they want to see you they can, later on in the day.

Some people feel reticent about closing their doors because it might offend someone. Don't be one of those people, otherwise you'll never finish what you set out to do.

Avoid appearing overworked
If you want to advance in your career, land a lucrative contract, or simply gain the respect of your personnel, then you should always appear fresh and alert. This isn't as difficult as it sounds. There's no magic formula for staying fresh and alert when you're overloaded with work.

- *Exercise* We can't repeat often enough that exercise, far from tiring you out, increases your store of energy. So if you want to be more effective over longer periods of time, exercise. As a bonus, you'll also look a lot better!
- *Get enough sleep* You're probably aware that sleep is the barometer of our general state of health and mind. Read a book on sleep, and get as much as you can out of your hours of slumber.
- *Eat energy* You won't be fresh and alert if you eat fast food, junk food, instant food, etc. On the contrary. Take the time you need to buy wholesome food, and to prepare it properly — vegetables, fruits, eggs, dairy products and complex hydrocarbons (especially rice and noodles). Good food puts the colour back in your cheeks, helps you sleep better, and makes losing weight a lot easier.
- *Do relaxation and visualization exercises* You learned about them in a previous chapter. Spending a few minutes a day in your mental oasis is an especially effective way of regenerating your energy.

6 Be a good salesperson

It's important that a leader know how to sell ideas. So here's a summary of the main principles of selling.

Imagine that you are the product to be sold. Would you know how to convince others to buy?

In this book, you learned a few tricks about packaging and

presentation of a product. Now all you have to do is arouse the interest of your potential buyers, like any good salesperson does.

You don't think the desire to buy comes spontaneously, do you? If you do, you'd better take another look. People don't buy anything they haven't already been conditioned to buy.

Any salesperson who's ever taken a course in sales will tell you that the first step consists of telling the buyer what benefits he or she will gain, either real or fictitious, from buying your product.

Every time you have to sell an idea, a programme, a project, or whatever, look for an argument that characterizes what you have to sell. Observe advertising techniques for an understanding of how the principle works. Instead of selling a brand of beer, ads sell the pleasure of having a drink with friends. Instead of selling a car, ads sell the pleasure of impressing others, or of being the fastest dude on the road. And so on.

Now let's see what a good salesperson is like.

Portrait of a salesperson

- A salesperson is someone who is appreciated by others. S/he is easily approachable, optimistic, happy, and capable of having a good laugh with prospective clients, because laughter always forms a special kind of bond with people. We are much more attracted to people who can make us laugh — this has been proven countless times.
- A salesperson has the gift of conversation. Just like a leader, the salesperson knows that to influence people you have to compliment them, listen to them, and encourage them to talk about themselves. In this way, you establish confidence.

Also, if you want people to listen to you, control the intensity of how you speak. Too much passion makes people uncomfortable and results in resistance — people get the impression all you want to do is sell them something. This is exactly the impression you should avoid creating.

Too little passion makes you appear indifferent — if you don't believe what you're saying, why should anyone else? So look for a healthy balance that is simply a reflection of your sincerity.

- A salesperson knows how to express him/herself. To sell your ideas, you have to be able to express yourself clearly, coherently and calmly.

Try to improve your vocabulary every day. There are a lot of words in the English language that we're almost afraid to use because we don't want to appear snobbish or superior. Don't think that way. Take pleasure in adding new words and expressions to your vocabulary.

- Finally, a good salesperson has to be tactful. Someone trying to sell you a car, for example, doesn't start with a tirade of criticism against all other cars, because s/he doesn't know what kind of car you're driving at the moment.

Try to avoid controversial subjects, even if you think the other person doesn't care much one way or the other. You'll be wasting your time, and you risk arousing animosity in persons you're trying to win over to your side. Such efforts often result in the opposite of what you'd hoped for!

In conclusion, don't forget that to acquire personal power you have to follow all the steps outlined in this book, and that each time a step is accomplished, it must be merged with those which have come before. Each step forward is based on the one you've just taken. Ultimately, they all join together and form an indivisible key to attaining real power.

Through this power, you will be able to understand the psychology of the people you lead. Don't take advantage of them and benefit from their weaknesses or faults. Doing so would be unworthy of you.

On the contrary, base your authority on their strong points. If you help them become more competent and proud of their accomplishments, you will provide yourself with the first-class support you need.

By helping those you lead, you help yourself.

SUMMARY

By acquiring a magnetic personality, you have also acquired supporters. It will now be very easy for you to become a leader.

How?

The first step consists of being noticed, of emerging from your anonymity. By showing that you're different, you'll attract the attention of those in a position to confer authority on you.

Start by acquiring some special skill that few people possess. Next, work on being polite and respectful. People will appreciate you all the more for it.

Make sure you have effective supporters — this is the key to all personal power. Try to be more tactful and diplomatic in your relations with colleagues and subordinates. Be subtle when resolving problems, without wasting time. You'll get people on your side by having a positive attitude, listening to what they have to say, and showing them that you're interested in their problems and accomplishments.

Above all, a leader knows how to manage his/her time. Make a list of your tasks, fight the tendency to procrastinate, define your priorities, and try not to create the impression that you're overloaded with work.

Finally, learn basic sales techniques, because you'll have to sell both yourself and your ideas. The portrait of a good salesperson is remarkably similar to that of a good leader.

CONCLUSION

Your Success Belongs to You

'Nothing succeeds like success!' as the saying goes.

The potential for success lies inside yourself. All you have to do is learn how to use it.

Combat your excessive shyness, acquire self-confidence, regain your self-respect, build a positive self-image, and learn to love and be loved.

By developing your personality and acquiring the charisma you've always dreamed of having, the world will open up to you in all its splendour and beauty, not the least of which includes material reward.

Now that you're coming to the end of this book, you're probably already a slightly different person than you were when you began. You've opened your mind to change, and to improving your self-image. You're finally ready to embark on the path to success and personal fulfilment.

However, don't forget that patience is one of the conditions for the success of any programme of personal development. Don't try to go too fast. Advance step by step, and make sure you've completely understood the contents of one step before going on to the next.

Persevere, and don't get discouraged if at certain moments you feel you're at a standstill. Take a break before continuing with your course on charisma.

Be confident that you will succeed. You're the only one who can interpret what life has in store for you. Stop being deceived by appearances, and you'll become free, independent, master of yourself and of your destiny. You'll be responsible for your health and happiness. You won't fear anything any more, because you'll finally know that all the talents you were born with are there at your disposal.

Live with intensity, attract success, be happy and loved. Come out of your cocoon, and rise up to the place that is rightfully yours.